# WINNING

# SOCCER

## FOR GIRLS

# WINNING
# SOCCER
# FOR GIRLS

**THIRD EDITION**

**Deborah W. Crisfield**

Foreword by

**Bill Hawkey and Patrick Murphy**
Coaches, Varsity Girls Soccer
The Pennington School
Pennington, New Jersey

**A MOUNTAIN LION BOOK**

☑Checkmark Books®
*An imprint of Infobase Publishing*

**WINNING SOCCER FOR GIRLS, Third Edition**

Checkmark Books
An imprint of Facts On File, Inc.
132 West 31st Street
New York NY 10001

**Library of Congress Cataloging-in-Publication Data**
Crisfield, Deborah.
  Winning soccer for girls. — 3rd ed. / Deborah W. Crisfield ; foreword by Bill Hawkey and Patrick Murphy.
      p. cm.
  "A Mountain Lion Book."
  Includes bibliographical references and index.
  ISBN-13: 978-0-8160-7714-4 (hardcover : alk. paper)
  ISBN-10: 0-8160-7714-2 (hardcover : alk. paper)
  ISBN-13: 978-0-8160-7715-1 (pbk. : alk. paper)
  ISBN-10: 0-8160-7715-0 (pbk. : alk. paper)  1. Soccer for women.  I. Title.
  GV944.5.C75 2009
  796.334082—dc22                      2008050595

Checkmark Books are available at special discounts when purchased in bulk quantities for businesses, associations, institutions, or sales promotions. Please call our Special Sales Department in New York at (212) 967-8800 or (800) 322-8755.

You can find Facts On File on the World Wide Web at
http://www.factsonfile.com

Text design by Erika K. Arroyo
Photos by Patrick Murphy, Jim Inverso, and John Monteleone
Illustrations by Accurate Art
Composition by Hermitage Publishing Services
Cover printed by Bang Printing, Brainerd, MN
Book printed and bound by Bang Printing, Brainerd, MN
Date printed: February 2010
Printed in the United States of America

10 9 8 7 6 5 4 3 2

This book is printed on acid-free paper.

All links and Web addresses were checked and verified to be correct at the time of publication. Because of the dynamic nature of the Web, some addresses and links may have changed since publication and may no longer be valid.

# CONTENTS

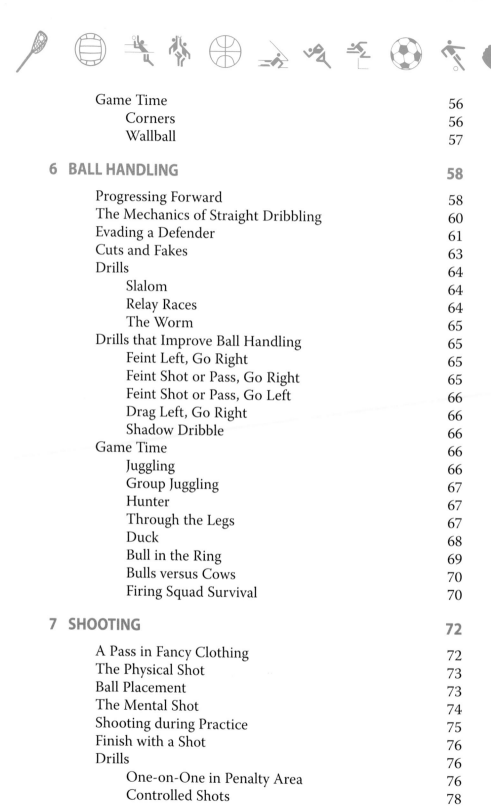

# ACKNOWLEDGMENTS

The author would like to extend a special thanks to the following people, without whom this book would not have been possible: The Pennington School girls' soccer coaches, Bill Hawkey and Patrick Murphy, and team; players Alexa Carugati, Chloe Deon, and Kaitlyn Kerr (photo below) who demonstrated the many drills and skills on these pages; and Jim Inverso, John Monteleone, and Patrick Murphy (yes, the same Patrick Murphy—a great coach and lensman), who contributed the photographs.

# FOREWORD

The appeal of soccer is no mystery. It resonates with the very essence of an athlete's physical abilities. Athletes who like to run find that the game rewards them for both their speed and their endurance. Young players who like to be part of a group and to accomplish a goal with teammates need look no further than a soccer field. It takes more than one player to move the ball down the field and score goals, and teamwork builds confidence and trust, traits that an athlete can use in everyday living.

The game is also easy to understand. Get the ball into the net. Accomplish this by using any part of your body except your hands. Soccer tactics can be straightforward and basic or quite complicated. Offense-defense mismatches such as three-on-two, two-on-one or speed versus size on a breakaway can decide the outcome of a game.

In soccer there is no huddling or timeouts to call set plays, only continuous action where players are required to think and make decisions literally "on the run." The action is mentally challenging. Players go from defending one minute to attacking the next. You cannot play soccer without being totally engaged—physically, mentally, and emotionally. What's not to love about an activity that so totally challenges you and keeps you alert and active on so many levels?

Soccer is a game in which an individual can improve her skills working by herself. She needs only a ball and dedication. Many an Olympic soccer champion has launched her rise to the top using a wall or a backyard. You don't need expensive equipment—only a ball, some imagination, and a desire to improve.

Long popular in the world, soccer has made great strides over the past 25 years in the United States. Today, girls' soccer is completely enmeshed in our sports culture, especially at the youth league, scholastic, collegiate, and Olympic levels of play. More and more young girls are noticing and stepping up to be part of the fun. It's exhilarating to be part of this growth and gratifying for us to have the opportunity to coach these aspiring athletes.

At the Pennington School we've produced championship teams and all-star players, including academic all-America selections as well as selections on the *Parade* magazine all-America teams. We've won the New Jersey state prep championships for girls soccer teams 10 times since our program began in 1982, and along the way have been consistently ranked number one among New Jersey private schools. Since 2002, our team has broken through with top-20 national rankings among all high schools in the United States of America.

We know that our athletes love competition and want to test themselves against the very best. They understand that preparation breeds confidence and confidence yields success. The first step in preparing is to learn how to play the game correctly, and to master the fundamentals. Our girls practice the skills needed to succeed on the soccer field each and every day of our season. We work on the basics and try to get a little bit better each day.

That's why we're pleased to assist in presenting the skills and drills on the pages of *Winning Soccer for Girls*, which is an excellent guide for learning the principal aspects of the game. Like long journeys, great athletic performances begin with a single step. You can take your first step by studying and applying what's in this book, such as the correct way to handle the ball, to defend, to shoot and to play as a team. It's all here on these pages. Start reading and becoming the best you can be.

—Bill Hawkey and Patrick Murphy
Coaches, Varsity Girls Soccer
The Pennington School
Pennington, New Jersey

# INTRODUCTION

## THE GROWTH OF GIRLS' SOCCER

Women's soccer has finally arrived. When I began playing the sport in the seventies, it was still "the other sport" to play in the fall. Most athletic girls, at least in the preppy suburb in which I was growing up, hit junior high and headed straight for field hockey, with its short sticks and short kilts. Many high schools didn't even have girls' soccer programs. Fortunately, mine did, and my devotion to the sport was off and running.

Right around this time, towns discovered that youth soccer leagues were a popular and inexpensive way to provide recreation for the area's children. A ball, a field, and some cones for goals were all that were needed, and at the youngest ages, boys and girls could play together. My sister, ten years younger, was at the right age to benefit from these programs, and by the time she reached junior high, her youth team had not only traveled all over the state for tournaments, but had covered most of the northeastern United States as well.

The opportunities were incredible, and before long these youth leagues had created hordes of young soccer players who grew into older players crazy about the game. These players have since invaded the high school, college, and Olympic levels.

The experience that girls gain from this early exposure to the sport is invaluable. When I played soccer in high school, interest was so slight that we only had a varsity team, and there were no cuts. Now many high schools have a varsity, a junior varsity, and even a freshman team, and the level of play rivals that of my former college team. Girls from age six on up have found a sport they love.

This shouldn't come as a big surprise. Soccer has, for a long time, been the most popular sport in the world. The United States is the only major country where soccer fails the popularity test. However, American women have embraced the game and won three gold medals in the past four Summer Olympics. Youth soccer leagues are going strong and the natural

appeal of the sport is working its charms. It's cheaper, safer, and (in many people's minds) more fun than the competition. Unquestionably, the best way for soccer to become number one in this country is for young people to keep playing it. Fortunately, they are doing just that.

Given that girls are spearheading this American soccer movement, it seems only natural that they should have a book written especially for them. And *Winning Soccer for Girls* is that book.

## A LOOK INSIDE

This book covers all aspects of soccer, from the rules of the game to strategies for winning, and it can be used by both the player and the coach. The chapters on skills detail the mechanics of passing, ball handling, shooting on goal, and heading, and describe the most opportune time to use the variations of each. Each of these chapters goes over the hows and whys of a specific skill and includes drills and games that you can use to improve your technique.

In addition to learning skill development, however, soccer players have to be in good shape. The book begins with a detailed chapter on training, covering warm-ups, stretching, and endurance programs. Drills and exercises that improve overall and soccer fitness are also included.

Following the chapters on skills is a separate chapter on strategy. In order to play competitively, you need to learn offensive and defensive tactics and how the skills can be combined in the larger picture of the game. When you put these mental skills together with the physical skills you have learned, you will have everything you need in order to play soccer to win.

## PRACTICE TIME

Despite the comprehensive nature of this book, you are going to have to do more than just read. Like any other skill, soccer ability takes practice, practice, and more practice. Knowing the mechanics behind a specific skill won't do you much good if your body can't execute it. Just like a one-year-old learning to walk, you have to train your body to move in a new way.

Keep in mind that practice can come in many forms. It certainly can't hurt to take a hundred shots on goal every day, but if that's too boring for you, try turning your practice into a game. At the end of each chapter there are descriptions of games that make practicing more fun. And you don't have to stick to just these games; you can also make up some of your own.

## PLAY THE GAME

This practice should also include game situations. It's one thing to learn each skill; it's another to execute your skills in a game situation. The pressures that exist in a game add a whole new dimension to passing, shooting, and ball handling. That's why it's so important for you to get out and play the game. It's only when you're on the field that you can really get to know how to play soccer.

To develop, you have to play every day, one on one or three on three. If you don't have an organized practice, play on your own. Don't worry too much about having a field with fancy goals; you can create your own in your neighborhood, your backyard, even your driveway. This is where you experiment to see what works, and this is where you develop a real love for

the game. Even though games are the fun part of the sport, keep in mind that games should always be combined with skill development. You won't be able to learn anything from playing if you start off with incorrect skills. In fact, a skilled player can learn tactics much faster than a tactically smart player can master the skills.

## THE MENTAL COMMITMENT

No matter what, though, get your head in the game. When you practice or play soccer, you should think soccer. Every time you're around a ball, your mind should be focused on the game. The minute you let your mind wander to the movie you saw the night before, the weekend's homecoming dance, or the total unfairness of your history teacher assigning a huge paper for Monday morning, you've lost the edge. Soccer should be your focus from the minute you start playing to the minute you stop.

This philosophy should not be reserved just for games. You should always practice the way you play. If you're focused during practice, then chances are you won't even have to think about focusing during a game. It will be second nature.

All this doesn't mean that you shouldn't have fun playing soccer. Actually that's the most important part. This is a game, after all, and you

# 1

# In the Beginning

## A SHORT HISTORY

Unlike the sports of basketball, badminton, or volleyball, soccer can't trace its roots back to a specific person, place, or time. In fact, it's completely likely that a variation of the sport was played in prehistoric times.

Generally it's believed that a game like soccer was played around 400 B.C. in China, and there's evidence of a similar game that was played in A.D. 200 in Rome. These games, while similar to today's soccer in the sense that there were goal lines and passing, didn't have the hand restrictions that today's game has.

During the Middle Ages, adults and children played a form of soccer in the streets of London, but the rules changed depending on who was playing, and so did the size of the game; entire towns participated. These games became so addictive and absorbing that in the 1300s the king of England actually tried to ban the sport because it was interfering with young men's military training.

Finally, in the 1800s, the game of soccer as we know it began to emerge. First the number of players and the size of the field got smaller. Then, in 1848, the first set of soccer rules was put down on paper.

Soon soccer began to spread throughout the world, taking Europe and South America by storm. In 1913 the Federation of International Football Associations (FIFA) was formed to link all the teams together and make sure that everyone was playing the same game. The most significant outcome of this new federation, however, was the establishment of the World Cup competitions. The first one was held in 1930 in Montevideo, Uruguay, and ever since then (except for a brief hiatus during World War

II), countries have gone wild for the contest, which determines the best soccer team in the world.

## WHAT'S IN A NAME?

Actually, most people in the international soccer-playing community would argue that the World Cup determines the best *football* team in the world. That's what the rest of the world calls the sport. The United States is alone in calling it "soccer." In the U.S., the name "football" is assigned to a somewhat more popular sport. (It's hard to believe that the name *foot*ball is actually used for a sport that is more of a pass, carry, and tackle game.)

The name *soccer* has its origins in England, believe it or not. When the official rules of the game were first established, the name of the game was association football, which was soon shortened to just football. But as rugby football developed, along with American football in the United States, the sport of soccer had to go back to being referred to as "association football" to distinguish between the sports. That was a mouthful, so it got shortened to "assoc," which eventually evolved into soccer. The nickname never really caught on in England, as rugby football soon became just rugby, but the new name was necessary in the United States, and "soccer" stuck.

## SOCCER IN THE UNITED STATES

The development and popularity of soccer in the United States has long been an uphill battle. After the North American Soccer League (NASL) folded in 1985 due to a lack of fan support, soccer seemed doomed in the United States. Over the past decade, however, it's grown in popularity and participation at a remarkable rate.

Hosting the men's World Cup in 1994 was a pure blessing for soccer players in America. It appealed to far more people than officials originally expected, and it even had a profound effect on the women's game. After winning the 1991 World Cup and then reaching the World Cup semifinals in 1995, the U.S. women's soccer team had already proved themselves to an international powerhouse. They were now focused on proving it to their country.

In 1996, Atlanta hosted the summer Olympics, and the hype stemming from the '95 World Cup brought Americans hope for a gold medal in women's soccer. By the time the Games began, women such as Mia Hamm, Julie Foudy, and Michelle Akers were household names to Americans.

Those three women, along with the rest of the women's U.S. soccer team, took full advantage of the opportunity to perform in front of their nation. They captured the Olympic gold medal in Atlanta, as well as the hearts and imaginations of young girls throughout the country.

Brandi Chastain's penalty kick rippled the back of the net and gave the United States a victory over China in the women's World Cup final in 1999; this victory reflected a major change in women's soccer forever. Approximately 650,000 tickets were sold to 32 World Cup matches held across America. The final game drew 90,185 fans to the Rose Bowl in California, a record attendance for a women's sporting event. Millions of thrilled viewers restlessly watched the event on their televisions at home, hoping that the American women would be crowned champion of the world's most popular sport—they were not disappointed.

Even before the World Cup, young female players had been lacing up their soccer spikes in record numbers: Approximately 5.3 million girls played soccer in 2007.

Thanks to the achievements of their predecessors, young girls can dream of someday becoming a professional soccer player. A women's professional soccer league, Women's Professional Soccer (WPS), has been formed and began play in the spring of 2009. The league consists of seven

# 2

# Rules and Equipment

ONE OF THE REASONS FOR SOCCER'S WORLDWIDE POPULARITY IS THE game's simplicity. The rules are not complicated and are the same whether you are in grade school or college, are male or female, or are from Brazil or the United States. Best of all, the equipment is minimal. With a few players, an open area, and a ball, a game can be off and running.

## THE PLAYING FIELD

Consistent with the diversity of the participants, soccer fields are not all the same size. The field has to conform to only a few minor limitations: It must be between 100 and 120 yards long, and can be of any width as long as the width isn't greater than the length.

The field is divided in half lengthwise by the center line, and this line bisects a 10-yard-radius circle that is in the center of the field. This is where the kickoff begins at the start of each half and after a goal is scored.

At each end of the field is a 24-foot-wide by eight-foot-high goal. In front of each goal is a six-yard by 20-yard area, called the goal area. This is where the goalie can't be challenged when she has possession of the ball and where goal kicks are taken. Beyond that is another rectangle that is 44 yards by 18 yards. This is the penalty area, and direct-kick violations within this area result in penalty kicks. This box also provides the goalie's limits: within the box she can use her hands; outside of the box, she is just another field player.

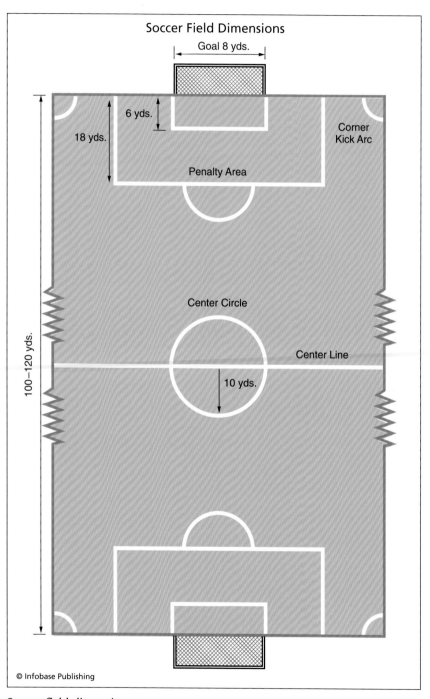

Soccer field dimensions

# THE EQUIPMENT

Besides the goals, the only other crucial equipment needed to play soccer is the ball, measuring 27–28 inches in circumference and weighing between 14 and 16 ounces.

In official matches, however, flags are also used. They are placed in the corners of the field to help the referees determine whether the ball left the field over the end line or the sideline in close situations.

Uniforms are fairly flexible, but they always consist of shorts, shirt, shoes—usually with rubber cleats—and calf-high socks. Some players also wear shinguards.

# THE RULES

The game is played with two teams of 11 players each. A team consists of 10 field players and one goalkeeper, who wears a different uniform to distinguish her from the field players. The reason behind this is so that the referees can see at a glance the one player who is allowed to use her hands. Once goalies have two hands on the ball, they have six seconds until they must release it. A goalie can take as many steps as she wants, as long as she stays in the penalty area. Many goalkeepers choose a flashy colored shirt with a wild design, hoping to confuse or distract the shooter when she takes her shot.

The object of the game is to be the team that scores the most goals during the 90 minutes allotted for play. Time runs continuously, except in the event of an injury or for some technical problem called by the referee.

The kickoff begins in the center of the field. Teams flip a coin to see who kicks off. Whoever does not kick off the first half will kick off the second half. During a kickoff, all members of a team must remain on its defensive half of the field until the ball is touched. The entire defending team also must remain outside the center circle. The first kick of the offensive team must go forward toward the opposing goal, and the player who makes the first kick is not allowed to touch the ball again until another player has touched it.

The ball is moved down the field by any part of the body except the arms from shoulders to fingertips. In order for a goal to be scored, the ball must be inside the goal and must pass completely over the goal line.

## Out of Bounds

If the ball goes out of bounds over the sideline, it is put back in play by a throw-in. This is the only time a field player can use her hands. The ball

Kickoff

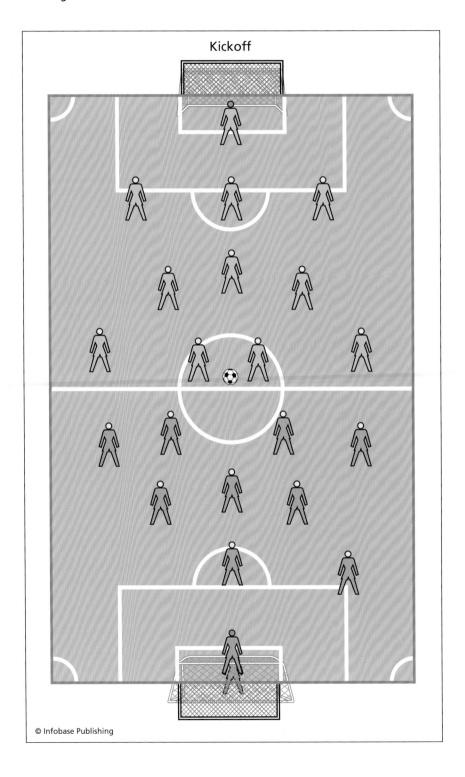

must be thrown with two hands, the arms must come straight over the head, and both feet must be touching the ground at the release. The ball is thrown in at the spot where it left the field. During throw-ins, a ball that is thrown and lands out of bounds is automatically awarded to the opposing team, even if the ball never crosses over to the playing side of the sideline during flight.

If the ball goes out of bounds over the end line, it is put back into play by a kick. If the offensive team kicked it out, the free kick is a *goal kick.* The ball is placed on the six-yard line and must leave the penalty box before another player can touch it.

If the ball is kicked out by the defensive player, the free kick is a *corner kick.* The ball is placed in the corner of the field on the side where it went out.

## Offsides

With the exception of the goalies, players are allowed to move just about anywhere on the field. The one exception to this is called offsides. This means that a player must always keep either the ball or two opponents (one can be the goalie) between her and the goal. This prevents offensive players from hanging out near the goal, waiting for a long kick to

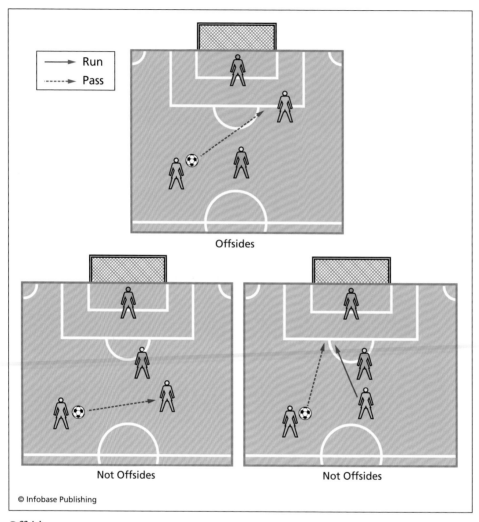

Offsides

come to them. You cannot be offsides on a corner kick, goal kick, or throw-in.

## Fouls

Fouls are called in soccer for kicking, tripping, charging, striking, holding, or pushing an opponent. It is also considered a foul if a player touches the ball with her hand or arm.

If a player commits one of these fouls, the other team is awarded a direct free kick on the goal. In many cases, this foul occurs too far away from the goal to be a scoring threat, but it is still an advantage to have a free kick.

If one of the direct-kick offenses is committed by the defensive team within the penalty box, then the offensive team is awarded a penalty kick rather than a direct kick. This is a one-on-one shot between a player of the offensive team's choosing and the goalie.

There are a few other fouls that are treated with less seriousness. These are dangerous kicks, obstruction, poor conduct, and offsides. These violations result in indirect free kicks. An indirect kick may not go into the goal until it has touched another player.

## A Few Unwritten Rules Too

The rules mentioned above are the ones found in an official rulebook, but it's a good bet that most coaches want their players to follow a few other ones, too. These are just a few guidelines that good soccer players adhere to strictly:

**No uncontrolled rebounds.** Every single time the ball touches your body, it should rebound with a purpose. There are only two options. The first would be to settle the ball easily on the ground in front of you. This will allow you to dribble it, shoot it, or pass it. You settle it when there is no defender on top of you.

If there is a defender, however, you have to go to option number two, which is redirecting the ball as either a pass or a shot. This can also be used if there is no pressure but you see a teammate making a great run or you see a wide open goal. It's often a less accurate pass or shot, but the speed you gain will usually compensate. Less accurate does not mean inaccurate, however. At no time should the ball just rebound wildly out of control. That is not soccer, it is pinball.

**Meet the ball.** It's harder to get control of a ball if you're running toward it rather than standing still, but nonetheless you must meet every ball on the run. Even if a pass is headed in a perfectly straight line toward you, you have got to rush in to meet it. If you don't, that perfect pass will be taken from you nine times out of ten by some defensive player who is hustling a little more than you are.

Even on the off chance that there's no defensive player in the vicinity, you should still make a habit of meeting the ball. Not only do you want this practice to become second nature, but you want to get to the ball as fast as possible to keep up your attacking momentum and not allow the defense to set up and wait for you.

**Support your teammates.** Soccer is a team game; therefore, even if you don't have the ball, you should put yourself in a position to be of help to other players. If your teammate has the ball and a defensive player is all over her, don't stand 50 feet away, calling her name, and casually observing the play. Make a cut; move in closer and let her know you're on the move with a call, "Back" or "Right." In other words, give your teammate some options.

This is also true even if your teammate is relatively open, dribbling merrily down the field. Support her. Follow behind, letting her know in a loud voice that you're available for a back pass, or cut down the wing, creating a wide attack and spreading the defense. If everyone on the team is in some way supporting the player with the ball, then the defense will have a tough time stopping the progress.

The same support rule applies for defensive players, too. If the ball is on the opposite side of the field, shift to the middle, so you'll be able to help out if the ball gets by your teammate. Anticipate the possible passes and movements of the offensive players.

Finally, "support your teammate" can also have an emotional component. Don't fall prey to cliques, petty complaints, or popularity contests. The best teams are unified teams.

Soccer is an easy game for a beginner to learn, yet it offers an enormous amount of intricacy and challenge for the more experienced player. That is what makes the sport so popular.

# 3
# Training to Play

SOMEONE ONCE TOLD ME THAT THE AVERAGE SOCCER PLAYER RUNS FIVE miles every game, much of the time at top speed. Unless you're a two-year-old with an unlimited supply of energy, you won't be able to withstand the rigors of soccer without some training. This means building endurance, building strength, and developing quickness. Basically, you're teaching your body to withstand the demands of the game.

But before any endurance or strength training can begin, a player needs to loosen up her body and get her muscles ready for action.

## STRETCHING

Before you do anything strenuous, including stretching, you need to warm up your muscles. Fifty jumping jacks or a short, easy jog around the soccer field should do it. You don't want to do anything too taxing, because you haven't stretched yet, but you have to do enough to get your muscles warm. You stretch your muscles to increase flexibility and minimize the chance of an injury during play, but if you stretch a cold muscle you may damage it before you even get on the field.

Stretching should feel good. It's designed to prevent pain, not cause it. When you start to stretch, take it easy. Stretch until you begin to feel a slight tension. This is the point where you should stop and hold the stretch for 20 seconds. As you hold the stretch, you should feel the tension lessen. If it doesn't, or if it increases, then you are stretching too much.

Once the feeling of tension lessens, you need to move into a deeper stretch. Push the stretch again until you feel the slight tension. Hold it

**13**

again for 20 seconds until, once again, the feeling lessens. The whole time you are stretching, you should remember to breathe and to keep the rest of your body relaxed.

Don't worry about how far you can stretch. Some people are just naturally more flexible than others. Eventually, you may be able to train your body to be more flexible if you stick with a regular stretching routine, but in the beginning, you should only stretch to the point of slight tension. Pushing the stretch to its limit will not in any way help you become more flexible. In fact, the opposite will more likely occur. Stretching done correctly will allow the muscles to move without injury over a greater range of motion.

Because there are so many muscles in the body, it's easy to overlook some. A tip for avoiding this is to get into a routine, working from the top of your body down or from the bottom on up. This will help you to remember which muscles you've stretched and which ones you haven't. The last thing you want to do is to forget an important muscle group. You only have to forget once and a bad muscle pull can put you out of commission for half the season.

Don't think you can skimp on the upper body muscles just because it's soccer you're playing. Even though the legs dominate the sport of soccer, your whole body still gets involved in every move, so you need to stretch all the muscle groups.

## Ankles

To start, rotate your ankles. Get them loosened up. This is a very vulnerable area in soccer because so much of the game involves footwork. After stretching your ankles, it's time to strengthen them. Rise up on your tiptoes 20 times in a row. The weight of your body acts as resistance. You should also feel this exercise strengthening your calves.

## Calves and Achilles Tendon

Now it's time to stretch your calves and your Achilles tendon. The mountain climber stretch is the best way to do this. With your feet flat on the ground, bend forward until your hands touch the ground, and then "walk" your hands out until you feel your heels start to lift. Allow one heel to come up and keep the other one on the ground; you'll feel a good stretch up the back of your calf. Now bend the knee of the leg you're stretching; you'll feel the stretch in the Achilles tendon. After one leg is stretched well, switch and do the other one. If you feel that your ankles still need some loosening up, you can rotate the ankle of the leg that is not being stretched.

The calf stretch

## Quadriceps

Now progress up your leg to the large muscle group in the front of the thigh. This is called the quadricep. To stretch the quad, stand up and

focus your eyes on a spot on the ground about six feet away. Lift one foot up behind you and grab the ankle. Now push your foot out until you feel a stretch down the front of your thigh. If you're having trouble balancing, make sure you're still focusing your eyes on that spot on the ground. After a good stretch, switch and do the other leg.

## Hamstrings

To stretch the hamstring, lie on the ground on your back. Keep one leg extended, and bring the other one up in the air so it is perpendicular to the ground. Keep the leg as straight as possible without locking your knee. Now push the leg back until you feel a good stretch up the back of it.

The quad stretch

The hamstring stretch

## Hip Flexor

The hip flexor is above the quadricep, running from the top of your thigh to your trunk. This happens to be a muscle many people never think of stretching, yet you can't even walk without using it.

To isolate it, get in a sprinter's crouch with your hands on the ground. Then extend the back leg out behind you as far as it can go and press the top of that leg toward the ground. The stretch you feel is the hip flexor.

The hip flexor stretch

The inner thigh stretch

## Inner Thigh

From the hip flexor stretch, it's an easy transition into an inner thigh stretch. Rotate your body toward your back leg. That back leg will go from behind supported by the toes to being supported by the heel. You should now feel the stretch in your inner thigh. Switch legs and do both the hip flexor and the inner thigh stretch on the other side.

## Hips

Now it's time to get back on the ground again into what's called the pretzel stretch. While sitting on the ground, with your legs tucked in neatly in your best "Indian style," bring your top leg up and over the thigh of the bottom leg. Now turn your body away from the foot and toward the hip of this top leg. Pull the knee into your body;

The pretzel stretch for the hips

The butterfly stretch for the groin

you should feel the stretch in the hip you are facing. Switch and do the other leg.

## Groin

The butterfly stretch is the best one for the groin. Once again, you're sitting on the ground. Touch the soles of your feet together and bring your feet in toward your body, trying to keep your knees as close to the ground as you can. Some people prefer to leave their feet out and then lean over, while pressing their knees down.

## Waist and Sides

To stretch your waist and sides, stand up with your legs about shoulder width apart. Lean to

Stretching the waist and sides

Stretching the shoulder muscles

one side far enough to make your ear parallel to the ground. Bring your far arm up over your head, keeping that in line with the ear as well. Do not lean forward.

## Shoulders

Unless you're a goalie or do a lot of throw-ins, stretching the arms is less important than stretching the legs. Nonetheless, you should still do it. To stretch the shoulder, bring one arm straight across in front of the body. Pull the arm back with the opposite hand, keeping the elbow stiff, until you feel the stretch. Repeat this with the other arm.

## Triceps

The back of the arm, or tricep muscle, is another good muscle to stretch. Raise the arm, bend the elbow, and then try to move the elbow behind your head. Do this with both arms.

Neck strengthening exercises

## Neck

Finally, because you're going to be heading the ball a lot, you need to stretch and strengthen the neck muscles. First, to stretch, press one ear toward your shoulder. Hold it for a few seconds and then press the other ear to the other shoulder. Now, keeping your neck extended and your head up, turn to the right as far as possible, and then back to the left as far as possible.

Once your neck is stretched, you can do a quick isometric exercise to strengthen it. Clasp your hands together with your fingers interlaced. Now place them on your forehead and press backward as you use your neck muscles to press forward. Continue to apply pressure for about 10 seconds, and then repeat the exercise twice. At the end you'll feel as if you can head the ball all the way down the field.

## ENDURANCE TRAINING

Once your body is loose, it's time to take off on a long run. Many sports emphasize the development of sprinting skills, but these skills aren't very important in soccer. The game, of course, does call for some sprinting, but it's minor compared to the need to run nonstop for 45 minutes while still maintaining the same level of intensity in terms of ball handling. Because of this, soccer players should be able to run at least five miles at a time very comfortably. Remember, that's about the distance you'll be running if you play an entire game.

It's hard to fit a long-distance run into every practice; there are too many other skills that need to be developed. Knowing this, players must take it upon themselves to get in shape before the soccer season even begins and then continue the endurance training on days when there isn't any practice.

Many coaches will have their players do some distance running at the beginning of practice or will set aside days devoted solely to endurance training, but that isn't enough. If you take on your endurance training yourself, you'll do more for your game than you can ever imagine.

# CIRCUITS

Because time is tight during practices, many soccer coaches like the efficiency of circuits, a series of exercises done together. A player can even develop her own circuit at home. Circuits build endurance and develop ball-handling skills at the same time.

A circuit should consist of about eight different activities. Each player (or group of players) starts at a different point on the circuit. Someone with a stopwatch, usually the coach, blows a whistle, and the players do the exercise at that station for two minutes. When the two minutes are up, the players move to the next station on the circuit, and accomplish the next designated task. The circuit ends when everyone has completed the exercise in all eight stations.

There are many options for circuit activities, and some are more rigorous than others. It's a good idea to alternate between exercises that focus mostly on fitness and ones that focus more on ball handling, so the players have some down time between spots. Here is a list of 10 exercises:

1. juggling the ball
2. sprinting through cones while dribbling
3. jumping over the ball
4. sitting down, throwing the ball in the air, standing up to catch it
5. toe taps on the ball
6. dribbling across the field
7. juggling with the head
8. push-ups on the ball
9. lying on back, rolling the ball back and forth under body
10. throwing the ball up, tucking your legs under your body as you jump, catching the ball.

# STRENGTH

Much of soccer, particularly the girls' game, depends on finesse and top-notch skills, but that doesn't mean that girls should ignore strength training. There are many times when players need to send the ball a good distance down the field, force a ball through a defender's foot, or throw the entire body into a head shot. Because of this, it's crucial to build strength in the legs, the back, and the stomach. Weightlifting is an obvious way to do this, but there are also a number of drills that allow you to do a lot of your muscle building right on the field.

Many of these strength drills involve a ball, too, which gives you that extra dimension of ball familiarity that you won't be able to find in the weight room. Keep in mind that even if you're not using the ball in a traditional soccer manner, you are familiarizing your body and your brain with the way the ball feels and moves, and every little bit helps.

## Crunches

The crunch is a form of sit-up that is especially good for developing a strong stomach for soccer. The player sits on the ground and places a soccer ball between her feet, raising it about six inches off the ground. Her knees are bent. Now she tries to touch her forehead to the ball. Once she has gotten as close as possible, she lies all the way back on the ground and extends her legs out. Then she crunches in again—15 more times.

Crunches

## The Rocker

The rocker is a good back exercise. When a player exercises on her back, she strengthens her stomach, so logically, if she exercises on her stomach, she'll strengthen her back. For the rocker, the player lies on her stomach, extending her legs out in back and her arms all the way out in front. In her hands she holds a soccer ball. Now she should stiffen her body, with her feet and the ball both off the ground, and rock forward and backward.

## Hill Sprints

The quadricep muscle, the one along the top of the thigh, is one of the most important muscles in soccer. It is crucial to running and is the source of the strength in kicks. It's obviously in a player's best interest to build up this muscle.

Hill sprints are the perfect way to do this. When you run uphill, your quad muscles are doing all the work. The more work they do, the stronger they get. If you can find a steep hill, sprint up it at top speed. Do this 10 times in a row about three days a week.

# BRAIN TRAINING

Good soccer play will not only exercise your muscles, it will exercise your brain as well. You have to learn to deal with the pressures, the anxieties, the fears, and all the emotions that you experience in a game.

Competing and coping with pressure are mental skills that need to be trained for just as much as the physical ones. You might think you have a skill down pat, but if you haven't practiced it under pressure there's no guarantee you will remember it when you finally face that pressure. When you're thinking about a million mental aspects of the game, your physical skills have to be second nature.

The best way to ensure this is to always reserve some part of your training session for just playing the game. And while you're playing, make sure that every practice session is conducted with the same intensity that you'd like to have in a real game. If you want to play hard and be aggressive and smart during competition, that's the way you want to train during practice.

Manny Schellscheidt, the men's soccer coach at Seton Hall University, thinks that brain training is even harder than body training. He remembers the first day he was coaching there: "I had no idea what to expect from the players. I decided to spend most of the practice testing their skill development. I had them play very demanding one-touch, small-sided games for almost the entire session. By the end, a couple of players came up to me and asked if they could just do some running. I couldn't believe it! I'd never heard of players who wanted to run. But what I had done was to force them to use their brains nonstop. They had had to be alert at every stage of the training session and now, mentally, they were exhausted. I sent them off on their run."

# DRILLS

These drills will increase overall fitness as well as many of those physical components needed to play soccer. No exercise equipment is necessary, but you will need a partner who is similar in weight and height and likes to mix it up a little—and have some fun—when training.

## Forward Roll

**Number of Players:** 3
**Equipment:** 2 soccer balls, 5 cones
**Playing Area:** field

The Forward Roll drill can be used during the conditioning portion of practice. Coaches like it because players work on sprinting (stopping and starting), receiving and returning passes, and improving agility. Players love it because it's fun!

For this drill, you need five cones and two soccer balls. Three cones are set up to form a triangle. The base of the triangle runs about 10 yards in length. The apex of the triangle is about eight yards above the baseline. The receiver starts at the apex of the triangle.

Two more cones are set below and parallel to the base of the triangle, approximately 12 yards away. Two servers stand at each cone with a ball (refer to the photo to view the set up).

To begin the drill, the receiver sprints forward to the left cone. The server to her left sends a crisp pass along the ground. The receiver traps the ball, sends an accurate pass back to the server, turns, and sprints back to the middle cone. She then turns to the right cone, drops, and performs a forward roll. The receiver gets up and continues running to the right cone where she takes a pass from the server. She traps the ball and quickly delivers a pass back to the server. She continues this cycle for 45 seconds.

## Push Up

**Number of Players:** 3
**Equipment:** 2 soccer balls, 5 cones
**Playing Area:** field

The Push Up drill is a variation of the Forward Roll. Again, this drill works on critical soccer skills but also strengthens the upper body. A strong upper body helps a player shield the ball from pesky defenders.

The cones and players are set up in the same position as in the Forward Roll. The receiver breaks from the middle cone and sprints to the left cone. Instead of trapping the ball, she makes a one-touch pass back to the server. She then sprints back to the cone and drops to the push up position. She does three push ups, gets up, and sprints to the right cone. She continues this cycle for 60 seconds.

## Leap and Roll

**Number of Players:** 2
**Equipment:** none
**Playing Area:** anywhere

One player crouches, head down, hands on knees, feet spread more than shoulder width apart, and legs bent at knees. Partner stands behind, then leaps over partner and continues into a forward roll. Partner stands and makes forward roll back to crouched partner, crawls through her legs, and leaps to her feet. Do 10 repetitions, then reverse positions so the other partner does 10 reps.

## Back to Back, Chest to Chest, Head to Head

**Number of Players:** 2
**Equipment:** none
**Playing Area:** anywhere

Stand facing each other, arms outstretched and hands locked with palms facing each other. Turn in the same direction so your backs are touching, then continue turning so you are facing each other again. Keeping arms extended and hands interlocked, push against each other, forcing arms to the side and bringing your chests together. Bring your heads together, touching at the hairline. Rotate side-to-side, turning hips but keeping hands locked and arms extended.

## Jump and Stretch

**Number of Players:** 2
**Equipment:** none
**Playing Area:** anywhere

Stand facing each other. Jump, chest against chest at the highest point of the jump; simulate heading back, left, and right (but not forward or you'll butt heads). Stand facing each other and lock hands. Slowly lower hands to touch each other's feet.

## Lift and Roll over Back

**Number of Players:** 2
**Equipment:** none
**Playing Area:** anywhere

Stand with a partner back to back with your arms locked at elbows. One bends forward lifting her partner off her feet. Repeat five times and reverse roles. Then stand back to back, holding hands over each other's heads. One partner bends forward at the waist, pulling her partner up and over her back and head. Reverse roles and repeat three times.

## Swing

**Number of Players:** 2
**Equipment:** none
**Playing Area:** anywhere

Facing one another, one partner holds the other behind the neck while partner holds her under armpits and swings her in a circle. Repeat five times. Switch roles and do another five repetitions.

## Fall, Catch, and Push

**Number of Players:** 2
**Equipment:** none
**Playing Area:** anywhere

Stand facing one another, one partner with arms outstretched parallel to the ground and palms facing partner. Facing player stands erect with hands by her sides and then falls forward toward her partner. Her partner steps forward with one foot, bending at the knee and lowering herself so that her hands are level with her partner's lower rib cage. Partner catches

Fall, catch, and push

the falling player just above midsection (her lower rib cage) and pushes her upright, palms extended. Or partner stands erect, arms extended, and catches falling partner at the chest alongside the shoulders (see photos). Repeat five times. Switch roles.

## Indian Wrestling

**Number of Players:** 2
**Equipment:** none
**Playing Area:** anywhere

Stand facing each other, the sides of each right foot touching, balls and heels of touching feet flat on the ground and each player's left foot placed behind with weight on the ball of this foot. Grasp each other's right hand. Partners push and pull, each trying to make her opponent lose balance and/or displace either or both feet. Wrestle five matches.

## Full Body Lift

**Number of Players:** 2
**Equipment:** none
**Playing Area:** anywhere

One player stands with arms straight alongside the body, hands balled into fists. Partner approaches from behind, grasps partner by the fists and raises the player off her feet. Repeat five times. Reverse roles.

The Stomach Toss drill

# GAME TIME

## Stomach Toss

**Number of Players:** 4 or more
**Equipment:** ball for each pair
**Playing Area:** anywhere

The Stomach Toss is a good warmup game that will help increase back strength. Players should choose a partner, and both players should lie on the ground opposite each other in the same position as in the rocker. The arms and legs are both off the ground, with the torso as the only contact point. There's a ball for each pair.

At the coach's whistle, players begin tossing the soccer ball back and forth to their partners. If they miss the ball or if their feet or hands touch the ground, that pair is eliminated. The last pair still throwing the ball is the winner.

## Over Under Relay Race

**Number of Players:** 12 or more
**Equipment:** ball for each team
**Playing Area:** anywhere

Players divide into two or more teams with at least six players in each team and line up one behind the other. The object is to pass the ball from the front of the line to the end of the line and then back again. The hitch is that the first handoff must go backwards over the top of the head and the next handoff must go through the legs. The first team to do this successfully is the winner.

## Leapfrog and Snakecrawl

**Number of Players:** 8 or more
**Equipment:** none
**Playing Area:** anywhere

This is a good conditioning and strength-building competition. Players divide into teams of four players each and line up one behind the other about 10 feet apart, with the first player starting on the end line. The rest of the players crouch low to the ground.

The player on the end line begins. She leapfrogs over the three other players on her team and then crouches down herself about 10 feet away. As soon as a player has been leapt over, she gets up and begins leaping herself. Once all four players have leapt over all their teammates, they turn around and stand up with their legs spread wide. The last player to do the leaping is now the first player. She heads back toward the end line, but this time she must crawl through her teammates' legs. The first team to have all its players successfully complete the relay is the winner.

# 4
# Passing

When the game of soccer is taken apart and each aspect is analyzed and rated, one skill stands out above all others. That skill is passing. It's the essence of the game, and a team that masters passing will master the playing field.

In sports that are played on small playing areas, the ability to pass is important but not essential, the way it is in soccer. Soccer's field is huge, and good passing is the only way to get the ball from one end to the other without the defense interfering.

Passing is a simple matter of transferring the ball from one player to another, and there are numerous ways to get this done. Passes can be short or long, and they can be lofted or on the ground. They can be passed from a near standstill, a quick ricochet, or out of the air. Despite all the different choices, however, all passes share a few basic traits.

## CONTROL

The overriding principle of passing is control. Many beginning players, not knowing this, think that power is what matters. You'll see a lot of them kicking the ball with the end of their shoes—which is called a toe kick. They often can send the ball a good distance this way, but they have no idea where it's going. That's no way to play soccer.

At all times, a passer must know exactly which teammate is receiving the ball and where the ball should be placed in order for her to get it. Any type of pass may be used to accomplish this, but the ball should go from a specific point A to a specific point B. Don't just kick the ball downfield, hoping that one of your teammates will pick it up.

This same philosophy of making the ball travel a specific path can be applied to the entire progress of the ball from its starting point (point A) toward the goal (point B). In this case, the "pass" will in fact be many short passes. It may seem like slow progress, but it's far more effective to use a shorter, controlled passing sequence of six passes than one faster long bomb that's up for grabs. The ball may be headed in the right direction at first, but your opponents are just as likely to pick it out of the air as your teammates. Before you know it, the ball will be coming back in the other direction.

# BEYOND CONTROL— THE REST OF THE BASICS

Once you've accepted the concept of controlled passes—and don't read on unless you have—there are a number of other areas to concentrate on to make your controlled passes successful:

1. **Look at the ball as you make contact.** Perfect foot mechanics won't mean much if you miss the ball.
2. **Passes should always be crisp.** A slow, lazy pass will probably be intercepted before it reaches your teammate, no matter how accurate it is.
3. **Lead your teammate with the ball.** You always want to send the ball slightly out in front of where your teammate is, so she can reach the ball without breaking stride. If you send the ball to exactly where she is at the instant you make the pass, she'll have to stop running in order to wait for the ball.
4. **Don't try to force the ball to a guarded player.** Sometimes it's tempting to try to get the ball to your best player, but if the defense is all around her, chances are the ball will be lost before it even gets to her.
5. **You don't always have to move the ball forward.** This is related to the last tip. If all the players ahead of you are covered, don't risk losing the ball just to move it closer to the goal. By passing to a player beside you or even behind you, you're giving the covered forwards an opportunity to get free, while still making sure your team has control of the ball.
6. **Don't telegraph your pass.** This is a difficult skill to master, but if you can, you'll be way ahead of the passing game. When you pass, try not to look at the player you're passing to. If you catch the defense off guard, you have a much better chance of making a successful pass.

Once you understand the basics of passing, it's time to decide which passes to use in different situations.

# THE INSIDE OF THE FOOT

The most basic and controlled pass is a short one done with the inside of the foot. Because of the nature of this pass, it's hard to get it to cover more than 15 to 20 feet effectively, but it does offer the advantage of total control.

To execute any pass, you must first take a step or a hop forward. You do this with the nonkicking foot, and it's called a plant. Let's say you are kicking the ball with your right foot. Your left foot is the planting foot. To make the pass, you want to plant your left foot on the left side of the soccer ball, about two to three inches away. The toes of this foot should be pointing in the direction in which you want the ball to go.

As you step or hop to plant this foot, your weight is forward and resting almost entirely on the planting foot. Your body should be almost directly over the ball. Now it's time for your kicking foot to swing through and contact the ball.

Your kicking foot should be cocked, with the toes pointing up in the air and your ankle locked. Your knee should be bent slightly, but all the motion for the kick is going to come from the hip. Swinging the entire leg, from the hip on down, contact the ball with the entire inside of your foot, heel to toe. You should try to hit the ball square in the center with as much force as needed to send the ball crisply toward your teammate. Make sure your leg continues in the direction of the pass. Do not stop your leg on impact. The follow-through will help maintain accuracy.

Using the inside of the foot to pass

Location of the planting foot for the inside-of-the-foot pass

# THE INSTEP PASS

The inside of the foot is good to use for accuracy, but it doesn't provide much power. For that, you need to switch to using the instep. The instep is the top of the foot—the part that is covered by the shoelaces. The instep kick is used more than any other kick in soccer. Because of the positioning of the kick, you can get a lot of power behind the ball, while still maintaining plenty of accuracy. The instep kick is especially good when you need to send the ball over a long distance, but it can be used for shorter distances, too.

To begin the instep kick, you want to take a slight hop toward the ball, off your kicking foot. You land on your planting foot, which will be on the side of the ball again, toes pointing toward the target. *This time the plant should be a little farther out, about four to five inches away from the ball.* Again, your weight is on your planting foot and your body is over the ball.

Now it's time for your kicking foot to make contact. Your toes should be pointed, with your foot extended—the opposite of the previous kick. Your knee is bent, and as you make contact, it should be directly over the ball. This will ensure that your pass stays on the ground. Like the inside-of-the-foot kick, the instep kick also gets much of its power from the hip, but it also adds power from the snap of the knee at the moment of impact. Your leg and your foot should be extended at the end of the kick.

The instep pass

Some players make the mistake of hitting the ball and then pulling their leg back, as if the ball were hot. This is a mistake. You need to follow through with the bottom half of the leg.

The contact point on your foot is your shoelace. This is the most rigid part of the foot, and it acts like a baseball bat when it contacts the ball. Don't make the mistake of trying to hit the ball down in the flexible area near your toes. You'll lose both accuracy and power because the surface will give a little.

When you kick, the ball should be hit square in the center, both left to right and top to bottom. Top to bottom is easy. If you make sure your knee is over the ball, it will be hard to get underneath it, so you just have to be careful not to top the ball. Right to left centering is a little more difficult. If

Keep your knee over the ball to keep the ball on the ground

Keep your planting foot four to five inches from the ball for the instep pass

you hit the ball on either side, it will have spin, and generally, you're not going to want this to happen.

There are times, however, when you will want the ball to curve in or out, and you should practice kicking the ball with spin so you'll be comfortable using it.

## THE LOFTED PASS

While a pass in the air is much harder for the receiver to get under control, there are times when it's necessary to use it. For instance, if you see your teammate flying down the sideline, wide open for a pass, you want to get it to her. If you pass it along the ground, it might be intercepted by someone on defense standing between you and your teammate. A lofted pass is the perfect weapon to use. You send the ball over the heads of the defense, intending for it to land just in front of your running teammate.

To make this type of pass you want to use your instep again, but you'll need to place your feet and your body in different positions. You also have to make sure that the ball starts out a little farther in front of you, which means you won't be able to protect the ball as much just before you make the kick. That's something to consider before you decide to use this kick.

As before, you are going to take a hop off your kicking foot before the kick. In this case, it will be a fairly big one, in order to give your kick the extra power that comes from your body's momentum. When you land this time, however, your planting foot will be much farther away from the ball. Depending on what's comfortable for you, your planting foot should be about eight to 12 inches away, and this time it's not up next to the side of the ball. The planting foot should still be off to the side, but it should be further back. If you drew a line across the toe of the foot, it would eventually touch the back of the ball.

Bring your knee back to loft the ball

The weight of your body is still on your planting foot, but it's all on the heel of the foot, forcing you to lean backwards as you kick, rather than forward over the ball. Your knee is still bent when the foot comes in contact with the ball, but like the body, it is also behind the ball rather than over it.

The contact point on the ball is lower. Try to center your instep on the ball, but on the bottom side. This is what will give it the loft. Believe it or not, if your planting foot is behind, your body is leaning back, and your knee is behind the ball, it is almost unnecessary to think about your foot placement. These positions will practically force your foot to hit on the underside of the ball.

## THE CHIP

You might think the chip would be similar to the lofted ball, since both of these passes are airborne. But because the chip is used specifically for short passes, the approach is closer to a grounded pass. You want to bring your planting foot closer to the ball again—alongside it rather than behind it—and your body should be leaning forward, not backward.

The kick, on the other hand, is the part that is similar to the lofted pass. Your foot should contact the soccer ball as far underneath it as possible. This is what will give it the loft. Because your approach tends to make this type of contact somewhat awkward, the ball will not have the power that a lofted ball has. The ball will pop up into the air about 10 or 15 feet: a perfect chip.

## THE VOLLEY

The volley is a pass that never touches the ground. The ball flies in the air toward a player. That player, using the instep of her foot, contacts the ball while it is still in the air and sends it on another airborne trip to a teammate. The volley is generally used more often during shooting than passing, but it can be a good passing option, which is why it's included in this chapter.

To execute the volley, you want to bring your knee up, keeping your toes pointed toward the ground. The ball must come directly off the instep, not the toes (which will cost you accuracy) or the side of the foot (which will cost you power).

The volley

# THE DROP KICK

The drop kick is also called the half volley. It involves practically the same move as the volley, but the ball bounces first, instead of being kicked by the player while it is still in the air.

0 The drop kick shouldn't be attempted until a player is comfortable with the volley. Timing is key to the drop kick, so that's what a player should be concentrating on, not the mechanics of the pass.

Essentially, the drop kick is the same as the volley. The knee is up and the toes are down. The kick is done with the instep. This time, however, the player lets the ball hit the ground; then, in the split second when it starts to rebound back up, the player kicks it. The nice thing about this kick is that players don't catch their toes on the ground, the way they often do with instep kicks. The bad thing, though, is that a player's timing often will be off, and the ball will be hit with the shins. It just takes practice.

# THE OUTSIDE OF THE FOOT

Sometimes the ball needs just a little nudge over to an unguarded teammate. While this can be done easily with the inside of the foot, you have another option: Hit it with the outside of the foot. This pass requires just a quick flick of the ankle. It doesn't have much power, but it does have the advantage of allowing you to keep your body between the ball and the defender and still make a pass.

Using the outside of your foot to pass

# ONE-TOUCH PASSING

Most of the time you will want to bring the ball under control before you pass it off. This will ensure a good pass and will allow you to choose the best option for what to do next. Sometimes, however, you're not going to have that luxury. That's when you use the one-touch pass.

The one-touch pass is exactly what it sounds like: The ball is coming toward you and you touch it once, sending it in another direction. The one-touch pass is generally used in one of two situations:

1. When a defensive player is all over you and you may lose the ball if you try to bring it under control, or
2. When a teammate is making a great run and is open to receive the ball if you can pass it to her as quickly as possible.

Executing a controlled one-touch pass isn't easy. Some players, especially the defensive ones, will wind up and boot the ball as hard as they can. Because the ball has momentum when it's rolling toward the player, it will really soar. This may seem like a good idea for clearing the ball out of the defensive zone, but that's not always the case. It won't be a controlled pass, and chances are it will just go to the other team. They'll boot it back, and the game will look more like pinball than soccer.

A better alternative is to top the ball slightly when you hit it. This will take some of the power off the ball and keep it on the ground, allowing you to direct the ball to your teammate.

# DRILLS

To practice the kicks we've just described, you can use a wall, another player, or several other players. No matter how you practice, though, you need to remember that you should train the same way you would be playing in a game. In other words, don't just stand around and pass back and forth; you'll never come across this situation during a game. Move around. Make your passes on the run. Make some of them one-touch passes and bring others under control.

Once you're comfortable with the different types of passes, play a game. This is the only way that you'll be able to make your passing choices second nature. You won't have time in the middle of a game to stop and run through the list mentally to choose what's appropriate. But if you play enough, your mind will be able to make the choice before you're even conscious of it.

## Wall Kicking

A wall is a great tool to use in practicing passing. You can do it any time by yourself, and you don't have to worry about your partner getting bored with the particular type of kick you want to work on. If you want to spend an hour just on the chip, you can.

The wall is also the best way to practice the volley and the drop kick. Drop the ball out of your hands and kick it with the instep to the wall. If you do it correctly, the ball will be hit cleanly and solidly and will come straight back to you without bouncing. If you miss your instep, then you'll probably have to chase the ball. It's a nice incentive to make sure you execute the kicks correctly.

## The Weave

The weave is a three-person passing drill that helps players learn to move into the open spaces to receive a pass, and it helps passers learn to lead their teammates with the ball.

Divide the field into three lanes. Players should stand on the end line, one in each lane. The center person has the ball. She takes a

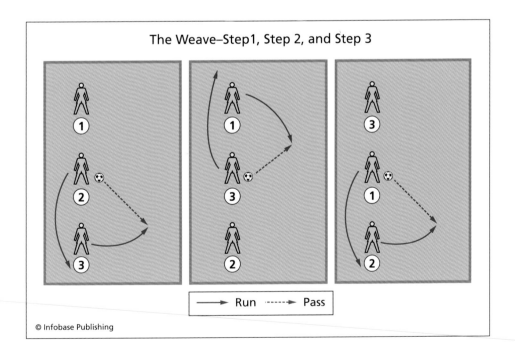

The Weave–Step1, Step 2, and Step 3

Run ------- Pass

dribble or two and then passes it either left or right, leading her team-mate as she runs. The center person then follows her pass and runs behind her teammate. Meanwhile, the teammate has received the pass and moves to fill the middle lane. Once she is in the middle lane, she passes the ball to the third player, and then follows the pass to fill that lane as the third player comes to the middle. The drill should end with a shot on the goal.

## "Yes" Drill

**Number of Players:** 4
**Equipment:** 2 soccer balls
**Playing Area:** field

Throughout a soccer game, an offensive player has possession of the ball for approximately one minute of the 90 minutes of play. She spends the rest of her time resting or trying to get open. This drill works on off-the-ball movement (when she doesn't have the ball). The object of the drill is to touch the ball as many times as possible in one minute.

Two servers, each with a ball, stand 20 yards apart. Two players stand in the middle of the serv-ers. One girl is an offensive player and one is a defensive player. The offensive player tries to break free from her defender through a series of body fakes or quick cuts to a server. The server delivers the ball on the command of the offensive player who calls out "Yes!" Once the offensive player receives the ball, she must quickly one-touch the ball back to the server. She then tries again to break free of the defender and get open for a pass from the opposite server.

Go as fast as you can and see how many touches you can accu-mulate in one minute. After a minute, the servers move to the middle—one becomes the receiver and one the defender—while the original receiver and defender each become servers.

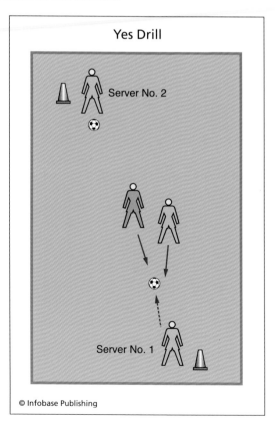

Yes Drill

Server No. 2

Server No. 1

© Infobase Publishing

## Windshield Wiper

**Number of Players:** 3
**Equipment:** 2 soccer balls, 5 cones
**Playing Area:** field

The Windshield Wiper drill demands quick, controlled passing with both feet. You often don't have enough time to control the ball in the game, so an accurate one-touch pass is necessary.

For this drill, you need five cones and two balls. Three cones are placed to form a triangle. The base of the triangle runs about 12 yards in length. The apex of the triangle is about eight yards above the baseline. The runner (or windshield wiper) starts at the apex of the triangle.

Two more cones are set below and parallel to the base of the triangle, approximately 10 yards away. Two servers stand at each cone with a ball (see diagram to view the setup).

The runner breaks to the left cone. The server on that side delivers a pass to the runner's left foot. She sends a one-touch pass with her left foot

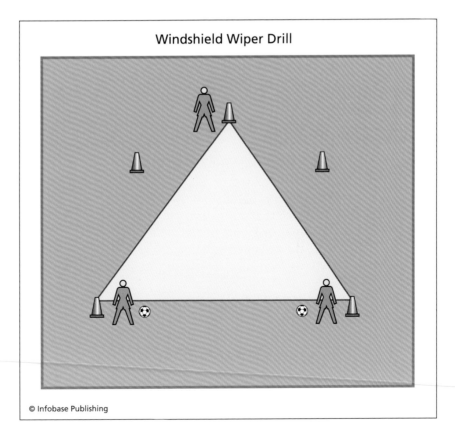

Windshield Wiper Drill

© Infobase Publishing

## Windshield Wiper Drill

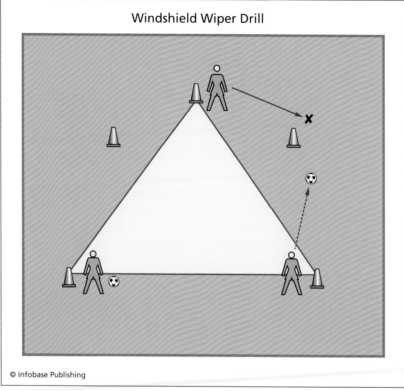

## Windshield Wiper Drill

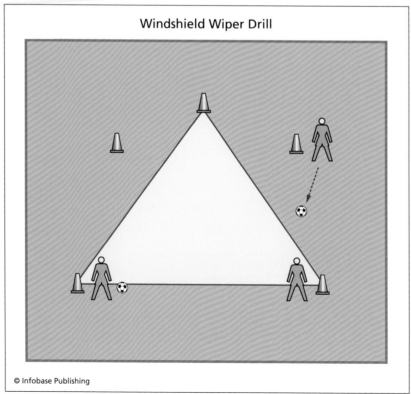

directly back to the server, turns, sweeps back around the apex point, and sprints toward the right-side cone. The second server delivers a pass to the runner's right foot. She quickly returns a one-touch pass back to the server. See how many times you can pass the ball back and forth in 40 seconds.

# Drills That Develop Ball Control

## Side Flick

**Number of Players:** 1
**Equipment**: ball
**Playing Area:** anywhere

Stand with the ball placed beside the inside of the right foot. Feint to the left by shifting your weight to the left foot while dragging the right foot to other side of ball. Flick the ball with the outside of the right foot. Shift your weight to the right foot and follow the path of the ball. Reverse sequence and flick the ball to the left with the left foot. Do 10 repetitions with each foot.

## Heel Flick

**Number of Players:** 1
**Equipment**: ball
**Playing Area:** anywhere

Stand with the ball placed beside the inside of your right foot. Feint a step forward with the left foot by shifting your weight toward imaginary defender. Bring the right foot to the front of the ball and tap the ball rearward with heel. Do 10 repetitions.

The heel flick

## Heel-Flick Fake and Go

**Number of Players:** 1
**Equipment**: ball
**Playing Area:** anywhere

This is a variation of the heel flick, and a good maneuver in traffic against an overly aggressive defender. Position yourself as in the heel flick, but fake the heel flick, swinging the right foot alongside the ball and to the back of the ball. Then tap the ball forward to left just ahead of left foot, which should give you clear sailing if your defender bought the feint to the rear. Do five repetitions.

# GAME TIME

## Six-in-a-Row

**Number of Players:** 6 or more
**Equipment**: soccer ball
**Playing Area**: field

If a player needs to work on passing skills, there is no better game than Six-in-a-Row. There are no goals in this game, which means that shooting and dribbling the ball are largely unnecessary.

The object to the game is for one team to make six consecutive passes without the other team touching the ball. Six consecutive passes equals one point. As you can imagine, the game will be as low-scoring as an official soccer game, because it is as hard to keep possession of the ball for six passes as it is to get it past a good goalie.

If the players are younger or less experienced, this game can be altered to fit their level of play by reducing the number of passes. Three or four passes in a row will provide enough of a challenge for novice players.

## Soccer Golf

**Number of Players:** 2 or more
**Equipment**: soccer ball for each person
**Playing Area**: field with cones or markers

Soccer Golf is good for developing a player's accuracy. Cones or other markers should be spread around the field, a good distance apart from one another. Players "tee off" and head toward the first marker. Players keep track of how many kicks it takes to get there. As soon as both (or all) players reach the marker, the player with the least strokes for that "hole" chooses which marker they will go after next. When all markers have been hit, the player who has completed the course in the least number of strokes is the winner.

## Hot Potato

**Number of Players:** 4 or more
**Equipment:** soccer ball, timer with a buzzer
**Playing Area:** anywhere

Every child has played Hot Potato at one time or another, but it can be adapted into a great soccer game to improve speed and control.

Players get in a fairly tight circle. They set the timer and then pass the ball to one another as quickly as possible. The player who is left touching or chasing the ball when the timer goes off is the loser and is eliminated. The last player remaining after all the others have been eliminated is the winner.

Instead of eliminating a player immediately, it is also possible to have a player spell *potato* (or a shorter word) before being eliminated—i.e., give a player a P the first time she is stuck with the ball, an O the second time, and so on. That way all players stay in the game longer.

## Ten and Again

**Number of Players:** 5 or more
**Equipment:** soccer ball
**Playing Area:** anywhere

The one player who is the target stands alone in the center of a circle formed by the other players. If she is able to survive 10 kicks without being hit, she stays in the middle and gets to try it again.

Players on the outside are allowed to pass to one another to get off a better shot, but they must yell "pass" first to distinguish the passes from the 10 kicks that the middle player must survive.

The person who hits the middle person is the next one to go into the center. The person who moves out of the center starts the play.

# 5

# Receiving the Ball

IMAGINE A SOCCER TEAM WHERE ONE PLAYER HAS THE BALL AND THE rest of the players stand around and watch her. Boring, huh? And not only that—it would be a ridiculously easy team to defend against. There wouldn't be any passing!

Now replace that image with one involving a team where the players are constantly on the run. The ball is moving quickly around the field, the defensive team is thrown off guard, and finally a beautiful, clear shot opens up. Now which image looks more like soccer?

Passing takes two, and if a receiver isn't in a good position, even the best of players will have trouble passing the ball. The ability to move without the ball is a skill that can be honed as well.

But movement is only part of receiving the ball. Most people aren't used to "catching" a ball with their feet. Toes, especially those covered by shoes, don't have the same gripping capability that fingers do, yet the soccer player still must "catch" the pass, whether it's coming out of the air or rolling along the ground. It's another basic skill that every soccer player must learn.

## CREATE OPTIONS

Theoretically, every player has three options when she gets the ball: She can shoot, dribble, or pass. But the ability to pass is nullified if there's no one in position to receive the ball. There's no point in passing the ball if it's just going to go to the defense.

It's also helpful if a player has more than one passing option. If there's only one person who can receive the ball, the defense will have an easy time stopping that pass, but if a number of players position themselves well, the many possibilities open to offense prohibit the defense from committing its players effectively.

In other words, when you don't have the ball, your main objective is to move to a position where you might be able to receive a pass. These five hints should help you open yourself to a pass more effectively:

1. **Keep moving.** It's much harder for defenders to stay with you if you keep them running. Make sharp cuts, and try to lose them whenever possible.
2. **Find the open spaces.** Often this means moving out wide to the sidelines or sprinting down the field. Distance yourself from the defense as much as possible.
3. **Don't bunch.** Just as you want to steer clear of the defense, you also want to stay away from your teammates. Your goal is to offer the passer as many options as possible, and if you and your teammates are all bunched together in the same place, that adds up to only one option.
4. **Be accessible.** Even though you want to move into an empty area, that won't help your passer if the empty area is behind two defensive players. You have to give your passer an open line to you.
5. **Know the passer's limitations.** Sprinting down the sideline can be a great break-free move, but if your teammate isn't capable of lofting the ball, it's useless. Know what your teammates are good at and react accordingly.

## PLAYS WITHOUT THE BALL

In addition to these five tips, there are several positions where a player should try to put herself in order to create passing opportunities. The word "position" here doesn't mean a specific spot on the field; rather it means the receiver's location in relation to the passer. These are some of the more common "positions":

1. Square
2. Wing
3. Wall
4. Overlap
5. Back

The entire team should know *and communicate these positions to one another.* You have to keep up the chatter on the field because your teammate may not always see you.

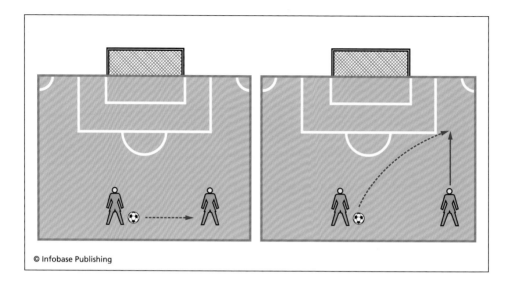

© Infobase Publishing

The names of these positions correspond to specific passes, though the names may differ from team to team. You want everyone on the team to be speaking the same language, so names should be agreed upon in advance. For instance, the "wall" pass is also called a "1–2" or a "give and go." It could get pretty confusing if one player yells "1–2" to her teammate when the teammate is expecting to hear "wall."

## Square

The square pass goes directly out to the side, with no progression toward the goal. Some players yell "square right" or "square left," but usually the passer will be able to determine just from the player's voice from which side the receiver is yelling.

The receiver should call "square" as she's approaching the square spot, not after she's already there, because the square pass is not one where the passer is leading the receiver. If the receiver yells it after she has already reached her spot, she becomes a sitting duck for the defense as she waits for the ball.

## Wing

The wing pass is also referred to as a sideline pass. The receiver cuts out to the edge of the field and sprints toward the goal, yelling "wing." Usually the passer will have to send a lofted kick in that direction to get it over the defense, leading the receiver this time.

## Wall

The wall pass is also known as the "give and go" or the "1–2" pass. The term "wall pass" probably came from indoor soccer, where players use the wall the way they would another teammate. In outdoor soccer, a player is going to use a teammate like a wall.

The wall pass is a good move to use to get beyond a defender who's blocking the way. It actually consists of two passes. In this case, the passer is the one who calls "wall." Then she passes to the receiver and sprints forward, beyond the defender. The receiver is in effect a wall that the ball bounces off on its way back to the passer. Of course, the receiver can help out a little bit by giving the ball a nudge around the defender and in the right direction.

## Overlap

For the overlap, a defensive player becomes part of the offensive force. Let's say the ball is with the left midfielder. The fullback on the left side will sprint from behind and shoot down the wing, yelling "overlap." (In some cases, it may be just as appropriate to yell "square" or "wing.") The defensive player should only try to do this, however, if there isn't already a wing player filling that space. Remember, you don't want to bunch.

The theory behind the overlap strategy is that it gives the team with the ball an extra player on offense. On top of that, the fullbacks usually aren't marked as tightly, because they're paired up with the opponent's forwards. This pass can shake up the defense and possibly create some openings.

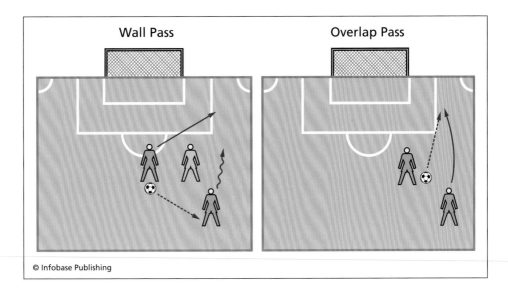

## Back

The ball doesn't have to go forward, and in fact, often it shouldn't. The back pass allows everyone to regroup. When the defense is heading forward, the person backing up the player with the ball generally will be freed up and have room to maneuver. This is also the perfect time to switch the ball to the opposite side of the field, where there might be less congestion.

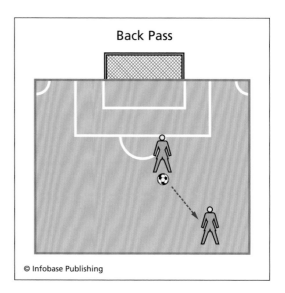

Back Pass

© Infobase Publishing

## Communication

Once you have labeled the different plays, be sure to use those names, because the passer will be too busy concentrating on keeping the ball to worry about having to do mind-reading.

And be specific. Just calling a teammate's name isn't much help. "Corinne!" or even "Corinne, I'm free!" doesn't give anywhere near as much information as "back." You have to be careful not to talk, though, when you're not free. If your teammate hears "square," she's going to assume there's a clear pass in that direction.

Keep in mind that talking isn't reserved just for those specific plays. Players should be communicating all the time. Tell your teammate when an opponent is coming up on her. Tell her when she has time to settle the ball and get control and when she has to get rid of it quickly. Since the player with the ball frequently has to keep her eyes on the ball and her immediate threats, her teammates have to tell her what's happening on the rest of the field.

# TRAPPING THE BALL

Now you know where to be to receive the ball, but how do you actually "catch" it with your feet? You can't, and because of that, you have to bring it under control in some other manner. The answer is to trap it.

Some people take the term literally. If the ball is rolling along the grass, they step on the ball just as it gets to them, trapping it between their feet and the ground. Or, if the ball is coming out of the air, they try to step on it at the moment of impact. While this method works, it's risky. Your timing

Trapping the ball with the inside of your foot

Trapping on the instep

has to be perfect or you'll be stepping on air. You also risk turning your ankle if you step on the ball the wrong way.

There's a better way to trap the ball that actually isn't a trap at all. Basically, you stick your foot out in front of the ball but without putting muscle behind

Trapping with your thigh

it. You let the ball push your foot back rather than letting your foot push the ball back. The presence of your foot will provide just enough resistance to take the momentum off the ball so it ought to stop right in front of you. If you try to offer more resistance than that, the ball will ricochet back where it came from rather than settling nicely at your feet.

The same principle works for balls both on the ground and in the air; it's the foot position that changes. If the ball is on the ground, you want to use the side of your foot. Your toes should be up and your ankle stiff. You should contact the ball slightly above the center. If your foot is lower, the ball will bounce up, and if it's higher, the ball might roll right under your foot.

For balls dropping out of the air, you want to point your toe and catch the ball on the end of your foot, not on your instep. As soon as the ball hits the end of your foot, you should pull your foot away and allow the ball to drop on the ground.

## TRAPPING WITH THE BODY

Sometimes the balls aren't dropping out of the air but rather are going straight through the air. In this case, you won't be able to use your foot to stop the ball, so you should use another part of your body, such as the inner thigh, the chest, or the trunk.

The chest trap is probably the most popular body trap for men, while the trunk is generally more popular with women. In both cases, you want to let your body give with the ball, so the ball won't ricochet when it hits you. Because this is harder to do with the whole body than it is with just

Trapping on your chest

Trapping with the trunk of your body

your foot, the ball will often rebound. To compensate for this, you need to try to run through the ball after the trap, pushing it in the direction in which you're going.

# ONE-TOUCH PASSING

One-touch passing was mentioned in the last chapter, but it's included here as well because players can use this option when they are receiving the ball. If you're in a wall pass situation or if the defense is all over you, you might not want to bring the ball under control. In these cases, you should think of yourself as a quick detour, rather than a pit stop, on the ball's journey toward the goal. With one touch, you redirect the ball toward a safer or more advantageous area on the field.

# DRILLS

## Receive and Continue in Same Direction of Pass

**Number of Players:** 1 or 2
**Equipment:** ball
**Playing Area:** anywhere or near wall

Do this drill with a wall or partner. Player receives a pass (off wall or from teammate) that approaches from the side. As the ball approaches, sidestep over ball with the foot closest to the teammate. Control the ball with the opposite foot; swing the outside of the controlling foot over the ball and flick it in the same direction as original pass. Get moving and follow the flicked ball.

## Middle Player

This drill requires three players and two balls. Players line up about 10 to 15 feet apart from one another. Each of the end players has a ball. The middle player is the receiver. The end player passes the ball on the ground to the middle person. She receives it and passes it back, whereupon she turns immediately to face the other player. This player should already have sent the next pass, so the middle person doesn't have to wait. She sends the ball back and turns back to the first player, and so on. After two minutes, the players rotate positions.

Once all three players have been in the center, the drill starts over, this time with passes coming out of the air. Now the end players should toss the ball, varying balls that go straight to the body and ones that are in a high loft that should be trapped with the foot.

If it's done correctly, this drill not only will build good receiving skills, but can provide the players with a great workout. The other advantage to this drill is that it forces players to trap the ball when they are exhausted. This is the way they are going to feel during a game, so they might as well create practice situations with those circumstances. Players will soon learn not to get sloppy even when tired.

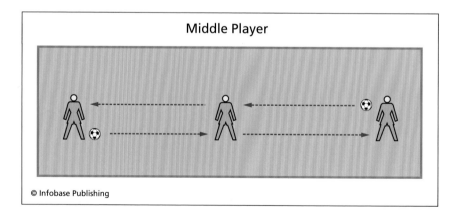

Middle Player

© Infobase Publishing

## Running Backward

In this drill, two players face each other, one standing on the end line of the soccer field and the other one positioned about five yards in, and prog-

The trapping-while-running-backward drill

ress down the field. While the receiver is running backward, the tosser is throwing the ball to be trapped. No matter where the ball goes, the receiver must bring it under control, drop it to her feet, and pass it back.

## Air Attack

**Number of Players:** 3
**Equipment:** soccer ball
**Playing Area:** field

The Air Attack forces players to trap balls under difficult circumstances. Once they master this drill, they'll be able to trap any ball. This drill also allows the goalkeeper to practice her punts.

Two players stand at the midfield line. One player is positioned on the right side of the field while the other plays the left side of the field. The goalkeeper then blasts a high punt to midfield. The nearest player calls for the ball by yelling "mine!" and traps it with her feet. After getting the ball under control, she sends a pass along the ground to her partner, who kicks the ball back to the goalkeeper.

If the goalkeeper's punts do not reach the midfield line, move the field players closer until they are within easy range.

# GAME TIME

## Corners

**Number of Players:** 4
**Equipment:** soccer ball
**Playing Area:** square with definite boundaries

Corners is a variation on the children's game of keepaway or monkey in the middle. In this game, however, the outside players are limited as to where their passes may go. This makes it easier for the middle person, although it is still three against one.

The three outside players take up position in three of the four corners of the square. The middle person stands inside the square. The outside people may only pass along the lines of the square, not across the middle. They also may only move along the lines of the square and not run across the middle.

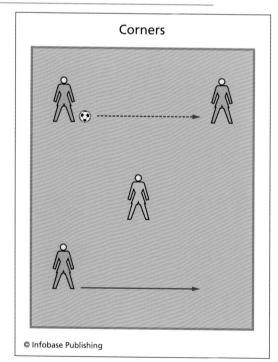

Corners

To facilitate the passing, a player should always have two passing options, which means that the players on the outside of the square are constantly switching corners. For instance, if the ball starts in corner 1, corners 2 and 3 are adjacent and corner 4 is opposite. The other players should be in corners 2 and 3. Then if the ball is passed from corner 1 to corner 2, the player who is in corner 1 stays where she is, adjacent to the corner with the ball, but the player from corner 3 must run over the corner 4 to provide the second passing alternative, because corner 4 is now the adjacent corner.

This game is an excellent way to help players learn to move into the open position to receive a pass. If the middle person is able to get the ball away from an outside person, she and the outside person who made the error switch places.

## Wallball

**Number of Players:** 2
**Equipment:** soccer ball
**Playing Area:** wall

As its name implies, Wallball is played against a wall. Two players alternate kicks in the air against the wall, each trying to create a carom off the wall that will be difficult for the opponent to field. Play continues until someone misses the ball or the ball hits the ground before it reaches the wall. The ball may hit the ground as it comes off the wall, before a player has kicked it. Each ball is worth one point, and play goes to 15.

# 6

# Ball Handling

Fake left, go right, touch with the toe, drag with the heel, move it up, and bring it back. Ball handling, otherwise known as dribbling, is a lot of fancy footwork that is used to move the ball down the field. Just as in passing, however, the ball never moves in only one direction.

Dribbling is one of the few skills you can practice well on your own. You don't even need a lot of space. Move backward and forward and side to side. Practice using all parts of your feet to control the ball. Use trees, lawn chairs, and bushes as "defenders" and try to fake them out by weaving around them.

Of course, if you do have a friend to practice with, take advantage of her, too. Unless she's very lethargic, she should provide much more of a challenge than a lawn chair. Start at one end of a yard or a field and try to get to the other without losing the ball to your friend. You'll be amazed at the fancy dribbling moves she will force you to create.

The more dribbling practice you give yourself, the better you'll be as an overall soccer player. Dribbling will help you get a feel for the ball that will be invaluable in other parts of the game, too.

## PROGRESSING FORWARD

The main reason for dribbling is to move the ball closer to the opponent's goal. But soccer dribbling isn't like basketball dribbling, where one player slowly jogs, bouncing the ball while planning to run a play when she crosses the center line. In soccer, everyone is involved, and the sequences are something like three dribbles, pass, pass, six dribbles, pass, four dribbles, pass, pass, and so on.

Don't interpret this sequence as a set play. When to pass and when to dribble is usually a decision determined by the defenders on the field, not by some predetermined plan created by the coach. Here are a couple of reasons why you would want to interrupt your dribbling in favor of passing:

1. **Evading a defender.** If you're dribbling down the field and a defender challenges, it's much less risky to pass the ball to an open teammate than to try to take on the defender one on one.
2. **Speed.** Let's face it: Dribbling just isn't as fast as passing. And if you're going to be a force in the game of soccer, you need to catch the other team off guard. The best way to do that is to move the ball quickly, and that means passing, not dribbling. So while you're dribbling, you should always be looking for that passing opportunity.

That said, there are also times when it is definitely best to dribble first and pass later:

1. **No one is challenging you.** Excluding the goalie, there are ten defenders going up against you and your nine teammates. If no one is

guarding you, then your opponents have the numerical advantage—ten against nine—over your passing options. If you can force one of them to commit to you before you send the ball away, this will even things up a little and hopefully leave one of your teammates open for a pass.

2. **A breakaway.** Occasionally, you'll break through the defense and be able to sprint and dribble a good distance, either down the center or, more likely, down the sideline. Because you'll be able to move the ball quickly and maintain control and possession, this is a better option than passing it off and risking the interception.

Just as the uses of dribbling vary, the techniques you employ will vary also. The ball handling you use to evade a defender is a far cry from the ball handling needed for a breakaway down the sideline.

# THE MECHANICS OF STRAIGHT DRIBBLING

The move-the-ball-down-the-field type of dribbling is the easiest. Essentially, it's just pushing the ball forward with your feet. It's a light tap, using the inside, the outside, or the top of both feet.

Most players tend to be more comfortable controlling the ball with one foot or the other, and most also seem to prefer a specific area of the foot.

Straight dribbling

Although this is natural, players should learn to use all parts of both feet in their dribbles. The direction in which you want to move the ball should be the determining factor, not comfort. For instance, if you want the ball to go slightly to the left, you should use the inside of the right foot or the outside of the left foot. Your decision depends on which foot your weight is on when you need to tap the ball.

There are two basic rules to follow for straightforward dribbling:

1. **Keep your head up.** The field is constantly changing, so it's vital to know where the defenders are and where your teammates are. Your breakaway might suddenly be challenged, and you'll be caught unaware if you're looking down at the ball.
2. **Maintain Control.** Even though you're sprinting, keep the ball close to your feet. If you're looking around the field, you'll only be tracking the ball with your peripheral vision. That means the ball needs to be pretty close.

A good rule of thumb is to keep the ball no more than one step away. That means that when you're sprinting, it can be a little farther out in front than when you're just jogging, but it still needs to be just one step, although a larger step. Anything more than that and you're practically giving the ball to the defenders. Many players think that if they kick the ball way out in front, they can sprint faster and therefore get to the goal sooner, but it does them no good to get to the goal quickly if they're going to get there without the ball.

## EVADING A DEFENDER

There will be times when you'll have to use your ball-handling skills to evade a defender one on one. This requires a completely different type of dribbling. You'll be moving forward, backward, and side to side, using the top of your feet, the soles of your feet, the toes, the heels, and each

Protecting the ball when marked

of the sides. Sometimes you'll move your feet without even touching the ball.

The key to this type of dribbling is protecting the ball and catching your opponent off guard. To protect the ball, try to keep your body between the ball and your opponent. This means you're sort of backing down the field until you can get by her.

Make sure you maintain contact with the ball at all times. Try dragging the ball one way, nudging it another way, stepping over it sideways and then tapping it back with the outside of your foot. Or step forward over it and then nudge it behind that leg with the inside of the foot. Lean one way and cut the other. Fake with your head and your body.

Everyone develops her own personal style in this kind of evasive dribbling, but contact and control are essential no matter what. The best way to master this type of dribbling is to practice using all parts of your feet so you feel comfortable switching directions in a split second. Work with another person and notice which moves are most effective.

## CUTS AND FAKES

If the defense is approaching but isn't right on top of you, you have a few more options. The best way to get around her will be to use sharp cuts and fakes. However, both the cuts and the fakes have to be convincing. A big, slow, loopy move isn't going to fool anyone. Here are a few classic moves to help you get by a defender:

1. **Cut back.** The first thing to look for is the defender's approach. Of course, if she's coming in fast at an angle, the simplest move for you is to cut quickly directly toward her, keeping the ball away from her feet. Her momentum won't allow her to stop quickly, turn around and go back in the direction from which she came. You'll slide by easily.

   This type of action is counter-intuitive for many people. Their instinct tells them to dribble away from the approaching defender. Unfortunately, this plays right into the defender's hands (or feet, if you prefer). Avoid making this mistake, because she has momentum working for her and can stay right on top of you.

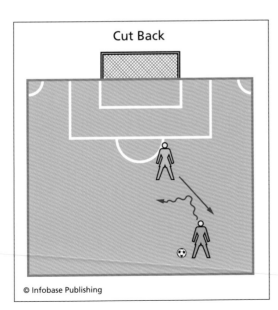

Cut Back

© Infobase Publishing

2. **Stutter step.** This is especially useful when you're sprinting down the sideline and a defender is right next to you. She's trying to prevent you from dribbling or passing into the middle, which is exactly what you have to do. Now is the time for the stutter step. Build up your speed and then stop. As soon as you have stopped, start running and dribbling again. This should put you one step ahead of the defense, allowing you to pass the ball into the center.

If your goal is to dribble rather than pass into the center, the stutter step changes slightly. As soon as you stop, drag the ball back slightly and make a quick, sharp drive into the center of the field.

3. **Rock and roll.** This is a good fake to use when you're backing down the field and a defender is between you and the goal. The first thing you want to remember is to keep your knees bent and your body low. You're going to be making a lot of body shifts, and you don't want to be thrown off balance.

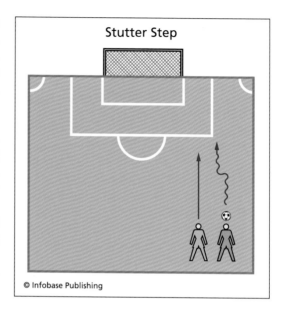

Stutter Step

© Infobase Publishing

First, back right into your defender, looking over one shoulder. Then rock your body convincingly in the direction you're looking, as if you're going to break that way. As soon as the defensive player commits to that fake, drag the ball backward in the opposite direction with the bottom of your foot, roll away from her, and head down the field. After you've done this a few times, you can make a double fake: Rock one way, start to roll the other way, and then roll back in the first direction.

# DRILLS

## Slalom

This is one of the easiest yet most effective dribbling drills. Set up cones or chairs or even sweatshirts (six is a good number) about four or five steps apart. Then proceed to dribble the ball through the course as fast as you can without losing it.

If you have a lot of people, players rather than cones can make up the slalom course. That way they can play a little defense as you try to dribble around them, forcing you to protect the ball the way you would in a game. When you're done, you become a post and give the ball to the next player.

## Relay Races

Any time you want to work on one specific dribbling skill, a relay race can make it more fun. For instance, if you want to work on using the outside of the foot, set up a race where that's the only type of dribbling allowed. This will also work for practicing such skills as dragging the ball with the sole of the foot or left-foot-only dribbling.

## The Worm

**Number of Players:** 18 (the entire team)
**Equipment:** soccer ball for each player
**Playing Area:** field

This drill forces players to keep the ball near their feet but also teaches them to change direction and execute sharp cuts at any given moment.

The entire team forms a single-file line. Allow for approximately 4 feet between each player. The first person in line, the "head" of the worm, begins dribbling, and everyone follows. The head is allowed to dribble over the entire field, which enables her to make as many twists and turns as she likes.

Players must stay in line and keep their ball under control. It's important that they keep their heads up to see the head's next move. The coach should allow each girl on the team to take a turn as the head of the worm.

# DRILLS THAT IMPROVE BALL HANDLING

## Feint Left, Go Right

**Number of Players:** 2
**Equipment:** ball
**Playing Area:** anywhere

Start with your body weight evenly distributed, the ball centered between your feet. Shift your weight to the left, step forward with the left foot, feint break to the left and forward while tapping the ball with inside of your right foot to left foot. Stop, pivot to the right (facing opponent), and flick the ball to the right (rolling the ball just ahead of the right foot). Make a burst of speed to move quickly past the defender.

## Feint Shot or Pass, Go Right

**Number of Players:** 2
**Equipment:** ball
**Playing Area:** anywhere

Feint a shot or pass with the right foot by moving the foot over ball. Draw the ball back with right sole and carry the ball to right side with inside of left foot. Sprint past defender.

## Feint Shot or Pass, Go Left

**Number of Players:** 2
**Equipment**: ball
**Playing Area:** anywhere

Feint a shot or pass with your right foot by moving the foot over ball. Draw ball back with right sole and carry the ball to the left side with the inside of the right foot. Sprint past defender.

## Drag Left, Go Right

**Number of Players:** 2
**Equipment**: ball
**Playing Area:** anywhere

Move the ball with the inside of your right foot to the left side, keeping the ball in contact with your instep or "dragging" the ball along the turf. Quickly plant your left foot and draw the ball back to the right with outside of the right foot. Reverse the move, dragging right and going left. Sprint past defender.

## Shadow Dribble

**Number of Players:** 2
**Equipment**: ball
**Playing Area:** anywhere

Each player dribbles a ball, the leader dribbling and the partner following. The second player executes the identical movements of the leader. Dribble 25 yards and return. Reverse roles.

# GAME TIME

## Juggling

**Number of Players:** 1 or more
**Equipment**: soccer ball for each player
**Playing Area:** anywhere

Juggling is the term used for keeping the ball up in the air, without touching the ground, by using any part of the body that is legal in the game of soccer.

The object of this game is to juggle as many times as possible before the ball hits the ground. Each time the ball touches a player's body it counts as one point. The player who can juggle the most times in a row is the winner.

If one player is juggling all by herself, she can set a goal and see if she can reach it in a certain amount of time, or she can try to beat her highest previous score every time.

## Group Juggling

**Number of Players:** 3 or more
**Equipment:** soccer ball
**Playing Area:** anywhere

For Group Juggling, players should organize themselves into a fairly small circle. One player lightly tosses the ball to the next player in the circle. This player juggles the ball as long as she wants (it might be only one juggle) and then pops it over to the next person in the circle. This continues until the ball hits the ground. Players in the circle decide whether it was the passer or the receiver who made the mistake, and that person is eliminated. The last player who is still juggling the ball is the winner.

## Hunter

**Number of Players:** 3 or more
**Equipment:** soccer ball for every player except one
**Playing Area:** anywhere

Hunter is another juggling game. All the players except for one have a ball, and they begin juggling them. The player without the ball is called the hunter, and she moves among the jugglers, distracting but not interfering with them. As soon as one of the jugglers loses the ball, the hunter tries to gain possession of it. When she's successful, she begins juggling, and the player who lost the ball becomes the hunter.

## Through the Legs

**Number of Players:** 4
**Equipment:** soccer ball, timer
**Playing Area:** anywhere

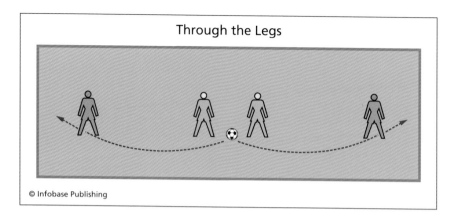

Through the Legs

Through the Legs is a workout that concentrates on developing ball-handling skills. Players split into two teams. One player from each team acts as the "goal," which she creates by standing about 30 feet away from the other "goal" and spreading her legs. The other two players battle it out in between.

A goal is scored when the ball goes through the opponent's legs, either forward or backward. There are no boundaries to the playing field. The "goals" may not move their legs in any manner to block the ball.

One of the "goals" (or a coach) should be holding a timer. After two minutes, the "goals" and the players switch. After all four players have had three turns each, the team with the highest number of goals is the winner.

## Duck

**Number of Players:** 8 or more
**Equipment:** soccer ball for each player
**Playing Area:** anywhere

Players, each with a ball in front of her, form a large circle. One player is the duck. She dribbles around the outside of the circle and then stops between two players. These two players take off around the circle, dribbling in opposite directions. The duck takes one of the players' positions and the person who dribbles the fastest takes the other. The slower person gets a D and is now the duck. When someone is the duck four times, and thus has spelled D-U-C-K, she is eliminated.

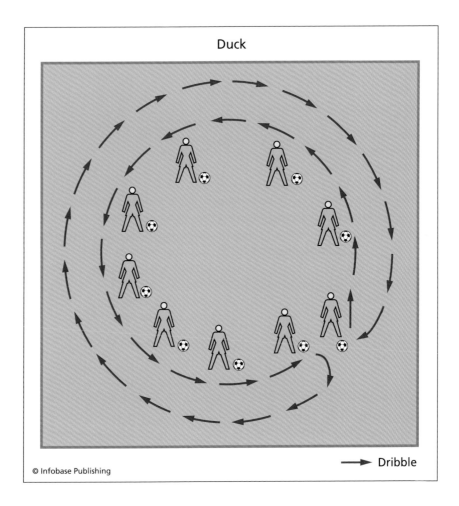

Duck

→ Dribble

© Infobase Publishing

## Bull in the Ring

**Number of Players:** 3 or more
**Equipment:** soccer balls for each person
**Playing Area:** field

The penalty box near each goal or the kickoff circle in the center of the field are ideal areas in which to play Bull in the Ring, especially with larger groups. Smaller groups might want to use half of those areas.

The object of the game is to try to kick the other players' balls outside the playing area. When a player's ball is kicked away, she must leave the playing area. The last player left with her ball is the winner.

This game is good for dribbling skills because players have to be in control, protecting the balls with their bodies, and looking up at all times.

## Bulls versus Cows

**Number of Players:** 4 or more
**Equipment:** one soccer ball for every two people
**Playing Area:** field

If there aren't enough balls to go around for a Bull in the Ring game, a modified version called Bulls versus Cows can be played. Players divide into two teams, the bulls and the cows. Each cow has a ball, but none of the bulls do. The bulls must clear all the cows' balls out of the playing area.

If a cow loses her ball, she is not eliminated; she stays in the ring and is available for a pass from another cow. Someone keeps track of the time it takes for the bulls to get rid of all the balls. Then the bulls and cows switch roles. Whoever eliminates the other team's balls the faster is the winner.

## Firing Squad Survival

**Number of Players:** 18 (the entire team)
**Equipment:** soccer ball for each player
**Playing Area:** field

Anyone can dribble a soccer ball from point A to point B; the challenge comes from maintaining ball control under pressure. This drill improves a player's awareness and forces her to keep her eyes and head up while dribbling.

Firing Squad Survival is performed best with many players (at least 11). The girls split into two single-file lines that are 20 yards in length and 10 yards apart. The players face the players in the other line. Imagine the way a basketball player runs through two lines of teammates after hearing her name announced before a game. In this drill, a player dribbles through that tunnel.

Each player in line (on both sides) has a ball. The dribbler starts at one end of the tunnel. Her goal is to dribble from one end to the other without losing control of her soccer ball. Here's the hard part: As she's dribbling, her team members kick their soccer ball at her ball, attempting to knock it away from her (see photo). The dribbler must keep control of her ball while avoiding the incoming balls.

This drill is fun to practice and even more fun to watch. If the dribbler makes it through the line without losing control of her ball, she's survived the onslaught of the firing squad.

# 7
# Shooting

THE WING CROSSES THE BALL IN FRONT OF THE GOAL. THE FORWARD rushes in to receive it. She settles the ball, but the defense is all over her. A quick dribble in one direction gives her an edge, and she sees her opening. Her foot flies back, then forward, and the ball sails into the upper left-hand corner of the goal. Score!

The shot is the glory move of soccer. All the fancy footwork, crisp passing, and tough defense that are crucial to good soccer play won't show up in the final scorecard. The only things that will count in the end are those few well-placed shots that slip by the goalkeeper. Shooting is the high-profile part of soccer, and everyone wants to be part of the action.

## A PASS IN FANCY CLOTHING

Despite its fancy trappings, shooting is really only a variation on passing. Precise placement of the ball is the key, though players often have a hard time understanding this. They think a shot must be a rocket ball, hit so powerfully that it puts a hole in the back of the net. That's really not true. The goal in making a shot is to place it just out of reach of the goalie, and this precision depends more on control than it does on power. A chip shot, a header, or a delicate tap away from the goalie will often be the best way to score.

The only real difference between shooting and passing is that a pass goes *to* a person (your teammate), while a shot goes *away* from a person (the opposing goalkeeper). Other than that, the same basic skills that are used for passing can be applied to shooting.

## THE PHYSICAL SHOT

Like the pass, the majority of shots will be taken with the instep. This shot provides the necessary power to get the ball to the goal quickly. Occasionally, however, a quick tap with the inside of the foot or a flick with the head will be all that is needed to score.

Believe it or not, it's your planting foot that takes on increased importance when you're taking a shot, because it's responsible for your timing, your balance, and your control.

If you remember from the passing chapter, the planting foot also determines the loft of the ball. Contrary to popular belief, when shooting, you generally want to keep the ball low. It's much easier for a goalie to reach up and block a high ball than it is for her to bend down to stop a low one. This means that when you plant your foot, you should place it up alongside the ball, forcing your knee over the ball when you strike it. If you do want a slight loft, however, move your planting foot a little more toward the back of the ball.

The rest of the shot is essentially a pass. Keep your eye on the ball and follow through with your foot in the direction in which you want the ball to go.

## BALL PLACEMENT

Once you've mastered the mechanics of the shot, where do you put it? A good rule of thumb is to draw a mental line one to two feet in from the sides and top of the goal and then put the ball between the imaginary line and the posts or crossbar. In simpler terms, you aim for the edges. While this may seem obvious since there's a goalie standing in the center, it's something that's easy to forget when you're in a game. People sometimes aim for the whole goal rather than a space within the goal, and the ball naturally heads straight for the center.

But not all edges are created equal, and the top choice for many players—the upper corners of the goal—is actually the riskiest bet. While it's true that these corners are tough for the goalie to reach, they're also tough for a player to hit accurately. Corner shots tend to sail out of bounds above the goal. A much better option is to aim low and go for the sides of the goal. That way if the ball rises more than you anticipated, you're still within range of another part of the goal.

As we noted earlier, another advantage to aiming low is that it is harder for a goalie to bend over or dive to stop a ball than it is for her to jump or reach for it. The high balls also can be tipped or punched right over the goal and out of bounds, while the low balls have to be handled more decisively or some shooter's foot will be on it to tap it in.

Areas to Shoot For (shaded area is target to aim at within the goal)

© Infobase Publishing

# THE MENTAL SHOT

Much of the skill needed for getting the ball to the edges of the goal will be training your brain to turn away from the idea of aiming for a target. There's a term used in the art world called "negative space," which means the blank area that is not the object in view. A soccer shooter would do well to train her mind to see the negative space.

Because of this, you really have to make sure your mind as well as your body is actively engaged in the game. While the mechanics of the shot should be second nature, make sure you are consciously thinking of where you are going to place the ball. Concentrate on doing the unnatural thing and go for the edges. You should know exactly where each shot is going to go before it leaves your foot.

Don't decide too early where the shot is going to go, however. You can't say to yourself, "lower left corner of the goal," before you know what the situation will be. Learn to think quickly as the situation unfolds so you can take advantage of the defense's or a goalkeeper's poor positioning. This will help you avoid telegraphing your shot to the goalkeeper, as well. As closely as you will be watching her, she will be watching you just as closely to see if you can give her a clue as to which way to commit.

Your brain should not only be noticing what the goalkeeper does in each individual situation; it should also be absorbing and processing the goalkeeper's reactions to all earlier shots. Figure out where she can go and where she can't reach. Watch to see if high balls or low balls are more difficult for her (usually it will be the low ones). See if she tends to favor one direction, and notice if she starts to commit one way before you even kick the ball. All these are clues that will help you score a goal, and you can't afford to ignore them. Getting the ball to the right place, whether it's a good kick or not, is the most important part of shooting.

## Shooting during Practice

Practicing your shot is not as easy as you would think it should be. Certainly you can take repeated shots at a wall to develop your accuracy, but that does nothing for your skills in reacting to the goalie.

And one-on-one shooting, with you and a goalkeeper, is only marginally better. This is an artificial, unpressured kind of shooting if there's no defense, and this situation doesn't happen very often in a game. It will certainly be a challenge for the goalkeeper, but it's not going to do much for the shooter. A player who practices this way will become too used to only having to worry about the goalkeeper's moves and will become distracted when she has defenders to deal with.

That's not to say that you can only practice shooting in a game situation under intense pressure. Limited pressure, in a practice situation, will do the trick nicely. Limited pressure means that the shooters outnumber the defenders by one; it does not mean that the defenders can slack off. They should be giving it their all, too. The offensive-defensive imbalance is especially helpful because it provides the shooters with gamelike pressure, yet it enables them to have more shooting opportunities than they normally would. This situation also allows you to step up the pressure once the shooters have had a string of successes. Add another defender to create matchlike conditions and see if the shooters can maintain their shooting skills.

Finish each drill with a shot on goal

## Finish with a Shot

Because shooting is such an important part of the game, it's a good idea to include it whenever possible. Even if you'e working on something else, such as corner kicks or wall passes, finish with a shot on goal. This will not only give players more shooting practice without doing a specific shooting drill, but it will also drill into their brains the convenient habit of always taking the ball to the goal, no matter what.

# DRILLS

## One-on-One in Penalty Area

**Number of Players:** 3
**Equipment:** ball
**Playing Area:** field with goal

The penalty zone in soccer is like football's red zone—the area from which the offense is expected to score. Here is a drill that simulates game action—a shooter against a defender and precious seconds to send a shot on goal. This drill calls for two players and one ball. The defender starts at the goal line; the shooter or offensive player takes a position just outside

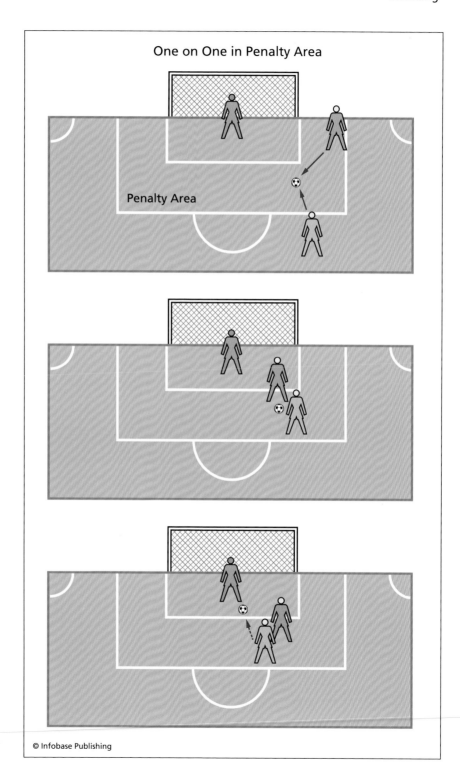

One on One in Penalty Area

Penalty Area

the penalty area. A teammate (usually the goalkeeper) tosses the ball into the penalty area. After the ball is tossed into the penalty area each player advances quickly to the ball, vying for control. The objective of the offensive player is to gain control and get off a shot within five seconds. The objective of the defensive player is to mark the player and/or clear the ball before the shooter can kick a ball into the nets. Play continues until five seconds elapse. Do 10 repetitions.

## Controlled Shots

**Number of Players:** 3
**Equipment**: 2 balls
**Playing Area:** field with goal

This drill emphasizes direction and minimizes power in shot making. Place one ball near the left goalpost along the goal line inside the goal (see photo). One player, who starts with another ball at her feet, stands 10 yards wide of the left goalpost, approximately three yards from the goal line. The other player stands five yards to left of the left goalpost 15 yards from the goal line. The first player passes the ball crisply along the ground to the second player, who moves toward the approaching ball and, without settling the ball, strikes the ball with her right instep—a short, blocking

Controlled shots

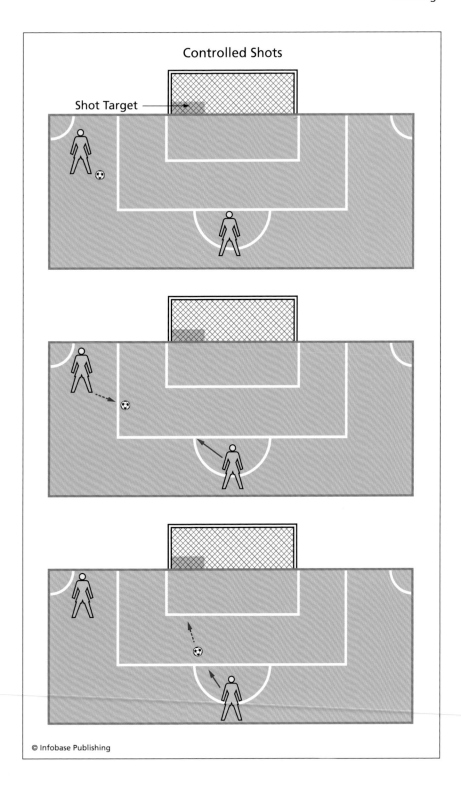

Controlled Shots

Shot Target

motion—into the left corner. The objective is to keep the ball low and on the ground, thus striking the target ball. All passes and shots must stay on the ground and the shooter must not blast the ball but should concentrate on control and direction. Direction and placement are more important than speed when shooting from near point-blank range. Goalkeepers cannot stop deftly placed shots that are out of reach. Reverse roles and repeat the drill from right side of goalposts.

## Serving Up Shots

This drill is as much a conditioning exercise as it is a shooting one, and it's one that most players love to do. Six or more servers, each with a ball, fan out around the penalty box. A shooter stands in the center. Then, one by one, the servers pass their balls to the shooter as fast as they can. The shooter must settle the ball and shoot or one-touch it into the goal. Servers should send a variety of balls in to the shooter—on the ground, in the air, fast, slow, bouncing, and so on. Once the shooter is finished, she switches places with a server.

While this drill doesn't provide the gamelike situation of defensive pressure, it does create the same intensity and urgency. The shooter is under the gun because as soon as she deals with one ball, another one is going to

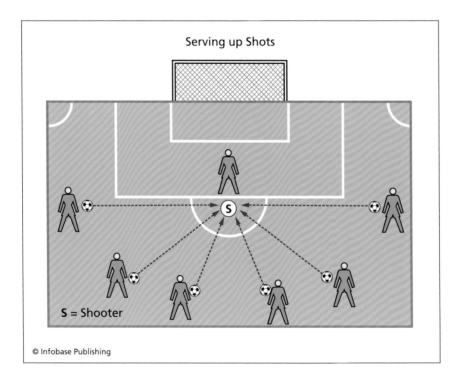

Serving up Shots

S = Shooter

be coming at her. She can't take time to set up perfectly, so the situation is close to what happens when defense is in the picture during a game.

## The Mini-Field

Another great drill for working on shooting skills is to reduce the size of the field dramatically. Provided your goals are portable, leave one goal where it's supposed to be and move the other one to the edge of the penalty box.

The teams should be four on four or five on five, and defense and shooting are the skills of this game. Passing and ball handling will be rendered nearly worthless in this drill because there is very little room to maneuver. Players on both sides will be forced to think "shot," which is something they should be thinking whenever they find themselves in front of a goal.

## Shooting on the Fly

**Number of Players:** 4
**Equipment:** soccer ball
**Playing Area:** field

This drill is for shooting a ball off of a cross while you're on the run. Soccer is a fast-action game, and you don't always have the luxury of getting your body and the ball under control before shooting. Sometimes you have to take your rips on the fly!

Shooting or volleying a shot on the fly

To simulate a game situation, the ball starts at midfield. Three forwards are set up: a right wing, left wing, and center forward. A goalkeeper is also in position.

The ball starts with the right wing. She sends a square pass to the center forward and then sprints down the right sideline. As the first pass is made, the left wing breaks diagonally across the middle of the field. The center forward gathers the ball and passes the ball ahead to the streaking left wing. The left wing one-touches a lead pass to the right wing (who is running down the sideline). The left wing then breaks for the right side of the goal. The center forward follows the play and breaks toward the left side of the goal.

The right wing sends a cross along the 12-yard line. One of the two players in front of the net attempts a first-time finish. After the shot, the next group of three begins.

A reminder to the right wing making the cross: Make sure you cross the ball out to the 12-yard line. If you cross the ball too close to the goal, the goalkeeper can come out of the net and intercept your pass.

# GAME TIME

## Four Goals

**Number of Players:** 6 or more
**Equipment:** soccer ball
**Playing Area:** field with four goals marked

If a player is looking for shooting and defensive practice, the game of Four Goals is a great choice. This is a variation of soccer in which each team has two goals, instead of just one, to shoot for. That means that the field has four goals, one on each of its four sides.

No goalkeepers are used, which means the goals should be kept fairly small. Players have to mark up player-to-player, which also works to develop defensive skills, because otherwise an opponent may suddenly reverse direction and head off toward another goal. The team with the most goals at the end of the playing time wins.

## Partners

**Number of Players:** 4 or more
**Equipment:** soccer ball
**Playing Area:** field with four goals marked

Partners uses the same setup as Four Goals, so it's often fun to play them right after one another. Each player has a partner, which means

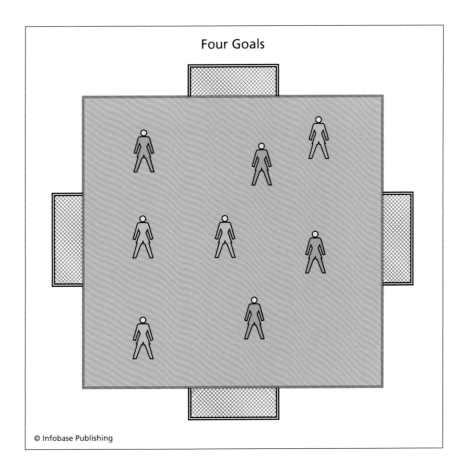

Four Goals

© Infobase Publishing

that, depending on the number of players, there could be more than two teams on the field at once—if there are six players, there are three teams of two.

The object is for a player to pass the ball through one of the goals to her partner. It can be any of the goals, and it can go through in any direction, but the partner must receive it after it has gone through. The partnership with the most goals at the end of the specified time wins.

## Knock-Out

**Number of Players:** 3 or more
**Equipment:** soccer ball
**Playing Area:** wall

Knock-Out is a great game for players who don't have much of a field, but do have access to a wall. Players get in a line. The first player kicks the ball to the wall and then runs to the end of the line. The second player gets the rebound and kicks it toward the wall again. Now she runs to the end of the line, and so on.

The rules of elimination can vary depending on the level of skill of the players, and the game can change depending on what people want to work on. If players are in close, they might have to kick the ball before it bounces. If they are farther back, they might be required to trap it once, and then kick, or kick it with no trap at all. If there is a line on the wall, the players might have to get the ball over that line.

Once the requirements are set, the players must complete the action. If a player is unable to do this, she is eliminated. The last player left is the winner.

## One Goal

**Number of Players:** 8 or more
**Equipment:** soccer ball, two goal markers
**Playing Area:** small field with goal in the middle

For One Goal, the playing field is divided in half, with a goal set up on the center line. The goal should be approachable from both sides. Players divide into two equal teams and then the teams split up so that half of each team is on each half of the field. Players may pass to their teammates on the other side of the line, but each player must stay on her own side.

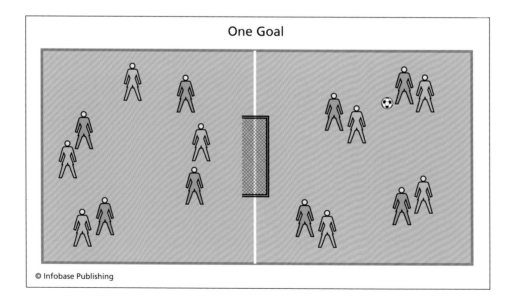

One Goal

The object of One Goal is to score as many goals as possible, and the ball can come in from either direction. It can get very confusing because both teams are shooting for the same goal, but a goal does not count unless it is clear which team took the shot.

## Feed the Dragon

**Number of Players:** 2
**Equipment:** soccer goal, 6 soccer balls, 1 cone
**Playing Area:** field

Divide eight soccer balls into two piles of four at midfield and place a cone on the 18-yard line. Two players stand on each side of the goal, facing midfield. The goal is the "mouth of a hungry dragon."

At the coach's command of "Feed the dragon!," the players sprint to midfield to retrieve a ball from their pile. They dribble the ball toward the goal and shoot as they reach the cone. After shooting, the players continue running toward the goal, circle around it, and then sprint back to get another ball from their pile.

If a player's shot misses the goal, she must retrieve the ball and shoot it again from the cone (at the 18-yard line). She may not get another ball from midfield until her ball lands in the net.

The players continue until all four balls are in the goal. The winner is congratulated, while the loser must perform 10 push-ups and 20 sit-ups.

Remember, shots must be crisp (accurate and with pace), as if they were shooting in a game. Players may not tap the ball and roll it into the goal.

# 8
# Heading

SOCCER LEGEND HAS IT THAT THE GAME'S DEVELOPMENT TOOK A macabre new twist during the Middle Ages. Apparently, players would replace the ball with the heads of people they had conquered. Perhaps this is where the concept of heading the ball began.

Whatever its origins, the headball has become a crucial weapon in soccer play. Any player who doesn't use her head in a game—both physically and mentally—is at a huge disadvantage. If the ball is coming out of the air, the head is the first tool you have in your possession to control or direct the ball's flight. And if you don't use it, especially in a crowded area like the space in front of the goal, chances are someone else will. Forget about trying to let the ball drop so you can show off your fancy foot skills. You won't ever get the opportunity.

Obviously, then, heading can be just as valuable as kicking, and it's a crucial skill for every good soccer player to learn. Unfortunately, many players (and, though it kills me to say this, high school girls are the worst offenders) shy away from heading the ball, often backing up to handle the ball with some other part of their bodies. Fear of pain is the big obstacle these players have to overcome, but the ironic thing is that a correctly executed headball will be as painless and harmless as a kick.

## STARTING OUT

The problem with the headball is that an incorrectly executed header *will* hurt, and when you are first learning to head the ball, more likely than not you're going to do it wrong. Unfortunately, these painful mistakes—face-balls, noseballs, scalpballs—are enough to scare players away from the header altogether. They never get to the point where they have the confidence to use it regularly. Don't let this happen to you.

The best advice I can give you to get through this initial painful learning process, and lessen the impact of faceballs, is to try using a softer, lighter ball at first. You also may want to start in close, heading a little tiny lob with no velocity, until you get the feel of where the ball should be hit. Otherwise your tendency will be to shy away from the ball, and this bad habit will be hard to eliminate.

# THE MECHANICS

No matter what your heading style, there are five basic steps to heading:

1. Get into position.
2. Watch the ball.
3. Keep your neck stiff.
4. Lean back.
5. Snap forward.

## Get into Position

Heading is a precision move, and a few inches can make a big difference. As soon as you see the ball heading your way, move left, right, backward, or forward to get in position. The ball should land right in the center of your forehead. If you're too far back, you'll end up with a faceball, and if you're too far forward, the ball will end up skimming off your hair.

## Watch the Ball

It is crucial that you watch the ball all the way into your forehead in order to prevent a bad or painful hit. It may be tempting to close your eyes, but resist the urge for the sake of your face.

Some players like to guide the ball down with their hands, as if they are going to catch it. This reminds them to follow the ball the entire way. This is effective, as long as you make sure the ball doesn't touch your hands accidentally.

## Keep Your Neck Stiff

Many people think that the head has to snap forward in order to deliver a forceful headball. This isn't the least bit true. The snap comes from the waist, and everything above the waist should be as stiff as a board.

Guiding the ball with your hands as if you are going to catch it

There are two reasons for this. The first is an obvious desire to avoid whiplash, which will most certainly occur if a hard ball flies into your wobbly neck. The second reason is to give the ball some punch. If your neck is loose, the momentum of the ball will push your head back, and the ball will fall powerlessly in front of you. But if your neck is stiff, the energy from that momentum will be transferred into the rebound, and the ball will fly forward with significant velocity.

## Lean Back

When you head the ball, all the force from your body should be generated at the waist. This is how you're going to get the most power. Some people try to jump into the ball, using their legs as the source of power; others

Leaning back before you head the ball

try to snap their head. Neither of these options will be as powerful as the snap of your body.

Because of this, you're going to have to lean backward as the ball approaches in order to give your body somewhere to go. If you don't lean backward, any snap of your body pushes the ball straight to the ground. Keep your legs bent to maintain your balance as you lean way back.

## Snap Forward

The final step is the snap. Using your entire upper body, which—remember—is completely stiff and leaning way back, snap forward and contact the ball with the center of your forehead.

You want to hit the ball on the center line or above it. The exact location depends on how you want to send the ball. If you want a sharp angle

Snap forward when you make contact

Hit the ball with the center of your forehead

to the ground, hit it more toward the top; if you want to send it on more of a line drive, hit it closer to the center. You don't want to hit the ball below the center line, however, or it will pop up in the air, losing much of its power and making it easier for the goalie or other opponents to intercept it.

## DIVING HEADERS

A diving header is the kind of spectacular, made-for-TV move that everyone gets to see on the highlight clips of a game. The ball is coming in low and would more likely be handled by a foot, except that the player realizes a foot won't get there in time. Instead, she dives toward the ball with her head leading the attack.

The contact point in a diving header is the same as in a traditional straightforward headball, but other than that and watching the ball as you make contact, there's not a whole lot of similarity. You can't possibly get in position, you don't lean back, and you don't snap your body. The dive will take care of getting you to the ball, and its momentum will provide the power.

Diving headers aren't too common, but they can be great weapons in front of the goal. If you know you won't be able to get your foot to the ball to kick it in, try diving for it. You can be pretty sure the goalkeeper will be caught totally off guard.

## HEADING TO THE SIDE

Once you've learned to hit the ball square in the center of your forehead, both standing up and diving, you're ready to move on to using the edges of your forehead to direct the ball to the side. Don't attempt this, however, until you're comfortable with the whole straightforward heading motion.

If you want to head it to the side, you need to lean your body to the side, rather than backward. From the waist up, you still stay stiff, but now you snap to the other side rather than forward. Contact the ball as close to the center of your forehead as you can, but obviously you will be hitting the ball slightly more on one side. Just make sure you are still contacting the ball with part of your forehead and not with your ear.

The sideways headball may be even more useful than the straightforward one. Think of a corner kick situation. The ball is coming in from the sideline and you want to get it in the goal. This is the perfect time to head it sideways. Also, if the ball is coming toward you, it's more likely that you'll have an open teammate to the left or the right of you, rather than straight ahead. No matter what, you should know what your options are and what you're going to do before the ball gets to you.

# FLICKING IT BACK

Forward and sideways have been covered; the only direction left is heading the ball backward. This shot can be used when you have a player right on your back, between you and the goal. You don't want to bring the ball under control in front of you, because you still will have to get past your opponent on your drive to the goal. Flicking the ball backward, sending it over her head, is a good alternative.

Another reason for using the backward head flick is to keep up the momentum. If you see a teammate making a great run, you can flick the ball to her with your head, rather than taking the time to get it under control and then passing to her with your foot.

The backward flick looks the same as a straightforward headball until the moment of contact. Then, instead of snapping the body forward, you flick just your head backward, contacting the ball on its lower half with your forehead. You're not really heading the ball; you're just keeping it airborne longer.

# GET IN SHAPE

No matter what style of heading you choose, you're still going to be using practically all the muscles in your body. The power of the hit comes from your stomach and back muscles. Your neck muscles are used to hold your head rigid. And your legs get you in position. Before you do any heading, make sure you are fit enough to do it well.

# DRILLS

## Head Forward–Head Backward

**Number of Players:** 3
**Equipment:** ball
**Playing Area:** anywhere

This drill needs one ball and three players, positioned five yards apart. Two players, one in the middle and one at the end, face the player with the ball. The first player tosses the ball into air, approximately 10 to 12 feet, toward the player in the middle and yells either "front" or "back." The player in the middle heads the ball in the direction of the command. Rotate positions after five repetitions until each player has a turn at each position.

Head forward—head backward *(continues on next page)*

Head forward—head backward *(continued)*

## Head–Chest Settle

**Number of Players:** 2
**Equipment**: ball
**Playing Area:** anywhere

Settling or controlling a ball that bounces to the height of one's chest or head is a difficult maneuver, but it can be mastered with practice. Here is a simple drill that will help. It calls for two players and a ball. Players stand approximately five yards apart, one with the ball in hand and one without. One player bounces the ball toward the other player, making the ball rise to at least chest height. The second player advances toward the ball, draws back her arms (to avoid touching the ball with the hands) and meets the ball with the chest or head, pushing the ball down and forward while moving, and settles the ball at her feet before reaching the other player. Do Five repetitions and then reverse roles.

## Holding Hands–Stand and Deliver

**Number of Players:** 3
**Equipment**: ball
**Playing Area:** anywhere

Holding hands—stand and deliver

Do this drill for three minutes and you're on your way to controlling the ball with your head. Three players (with one ball) stand holding hands, forming a triangle. Players head and juggle (tap ball with knees or top of feet) without letting the ball strike the ground.

## Sitting Heads

**Number of Players:** 3
**Equipment:** ball
**Playing Area:** anywhere

Three players with one ball sit with feet touching forming a triangle. Players try to head the ball to each other. Objective is to consecutively head the ball. Goal is double figures on each repetition for 10 repetitions. Make double figures every time and you're on your way to controlling the ball with your head.

Sitting heads *(this page and next)*

The Head Toss drill

## Head Toss

This is the most basic way to get players used to the motions involved in heading. Two players stand no more than five to seven yards apart. One player is the server, and the other player is the header. The server should throw underhand in order to ensure accuracy. The header heads it back.

Players should start this drill in a stationary position, just to get the feel of it. Then, as they become more comfortable, the ball should be thrown a little higher and the header should jump for it. Finally, the players should progress down the field, so they are in motion while they are heading. The server and the header should take turns after every 10 tosses or so to prevent headaches.

## Diving Headers

It's hard to get up the courage to try a diving header in a game, but if you practice outside of the game, this will become second nature and you won't even have to think about it. This drill is the best way to learn.

Again, there is a server and a header, but this time the header is on the ground in a pushup position. When the server tosses the ball, the header pushes with her hands and feet and actually leaps into the ball. Because they are already on the ground, players get used to the motion of a diving header without having to deal with the fear of the dive itself.

## Head Games

**Number of Players:** 4
**Equipment:** soccer ball
**Playing Area:** field

This drill is used to emphasize movement when you don't have the ball, aggressiveness, and heading the ball while an opponent is closely defending you.

Two servers stand 20 yards apart. Each has a ball. Two players stand between the servers. One girl is designated as offense, the other as defense. The offensive player tries to lose her defender through a series of body fakes and quick cuts. As soon as she sees the offensive player get open, the server tosses the ball high into the air. The offensive player must win the ball out of the air and head it back to the server. Once she heads it back, the offensive and defensive players continue covering and trying to lose each other. See how many times the offensive player can successfully head the ball in one minute.

Once the minute is up, the servers go in the middle and become offensive and defensive players, while the other girls become servers.

## Head Control

**Number of Players:** 2
**Equipment:** soccer ball, goal, 3 cones
**Playing Area:** field

Headballs can be used when you're defending, passing, or shooting. This drill teaches you to head the ball accurately.

The drill requires a goal and three cones. Set each cone on the goal line six feet apart. One player is the shooter and stands on the penalty kick line (12 yards from the goal). Another player is the server and stands a foot behind the goal line (inside the goal). The cones divide the goal into four mini-goals. The shooter gets three headball shots at each goal. First she begins with three consecutive attempts at the goal inside the left post. Then she tries to head the ball to the right and continues for a total of 12 shots. See how many goals you can score.

To make the drill more difficult, have the server vary her tosses. She can deliver balls to the left, right, high, or low. If it's a wet day, try a round of diving headers for fun.

# 9

# Goalkeeping

THE SOCCER GOALKEEPER IS A VERY DIFFERENT PLAYER FROM THE REST of the team for the very basic reason that she's the only player who is allowed to use her hands. She's high profile and can't be replaced on a whim by another player on the field. But unlike the singular positions in other sports, such as the pitcher in baseball or the quarterback in football, soccer's goalkeeper is not a playmaker. Rather, she is the last best hope when all else fails. A good soccer team should not rely on its goalie. If the ball gets that far, someone else hasn't been doing her job.

Nonetheless, the goalkeeper usually gets quite a bit of action during a game. She has to save the ball from going in the net, punt or throw it to her teammates, and direct the defense to help the team's cause. She always has to be alert, because the direction of the game could change suddenly, catching her defensive teammates off guard.

## PRACTICING TO BE A GOALKEEPER

Because the goalkeeper is a very different type of player from the rest of the players on her team, she needs to work on different skills when she practices. That doesn't mean, however, that a goalkeeper should have a separate session removed from her teammates. Instead, she should spend part of the practice session developing specific physical skills—including diving, falling, and punting—and the remainder of the practice with the rest of the team, working on her mental and tactical skills. If a shot on goal is the finishing touch on every appropriate drill, a matchlike situation for both the goalkeeper and the field players is created.

Goalies need matchlike experience as much as anyone. A goalkeeper who has a beautiful dive or a record-breaking punt won't be much good if she doesn't know where to stand as the ball is coming down the field. Playing the game is the best teacher for everyone.

## PLAYING THE FIELD

To take that philosophy a step further, every goalie should have some experience as a field player, particularly on defense, but offensive playing is helpful, too. If there are two goalies on your team—and every team should have a backup goalie—both of you should have time in the field when you're not in the goal. This will give you a better, more personal idea of how a defense moves to stop an attack. Knowing this will help you in numerous ways when you're back in the goal.

Punting

Rolling

Throwing

Drop Kicking

To begin with, you'll have a better idea about what players and areas your defense has covered and what areas of your goal are vulnerable. You'll also be more aware of when your defense is falling apart and what adjustments you have to make. Your offensive experience will tell you what options are available to the other team, such as when shots will be coming and which ones will be useless. Finally, you'll be more capable as the captain of your defensive unit, more knowledgeable when you have to direct your teammates.

## TOTAL FITNESS

While the ability to catch the ball is probably the most important trait in a goalie, the position requires a certain type of personality—someone who has a large supply of:

1. confidence,
2. mental toughness,
3. quickness,
4. physical agility, and
5. strength.

A goalie has to know when to charge forward to challenge a player and when to hang back to block a shot. She has to captain her defen-

Goalkeeper making save

Goalkeeper using two hands and getting her body behind the ball

Goalkeeper challenging a breakaway *(continues at top of next page)*

sive teammates yet never for a second stop watching the ball. She has to cover all corners of a very large goal and never, ever think for even a millisecond that she would rather not throw her body on the ground to stop a ball.

## STARTING POSITION

Before a goalkeeper can do anything, she has to learn the starting position. This is not described in soccer rulebooks, but it's the position that will allow her to be most comfortable yet still prepared to spring into action.

Her feet should be about shoulder width apart, her knees should be slightly bent, and her weight should be forward on the balls of her feet. This will save her a little bit of time when she has to spring into action. Her arms and shoulders should be loose but held out slightly to the side of her body, rather than dangling straight down. When anticipating a shot the goalkeeper must raise her palms up, facing the shooter. Most important, her eyes should be watching the ball the whole time.

Goalkeeper ready position

## NARROWING THE ANGLE

Now you're in the ready position, your defense has let you down, and you see your opponents dribbling the ball toward you. What do you do? The answer is *move*. Placing your body between the ball and the goal is the number one principle of goalkeeping.

If the attacker is heading straight down the middle, you probably are already in position, but it's more likely that the shooter will be coming in at some sort of an angle. Move your body to face that assault head on. It's called narrowing the angle, and it will cut off much of the open goal that is available to the shooter.

For instance, if the ball is coming in on the right side, you should move over toward the right side. Now there is very little net open on the right, and your body is between the shooter and the left side of the net, which makes it more likely that you will stop her attack. Isn't that a lot more comfortable than standing in the middle and diving for the shot? It's considerably easier and a little nicer on the body, too.

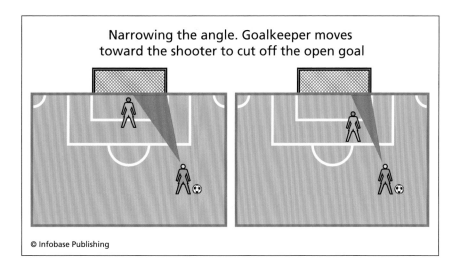

Narrowing the angle. Goalkeeper moves toward the shooter to cut off the open goal

© Infobase Publishing

Narrowing the angle has a side benefit, too. In addition to limiting the area in which the shooter can place the ball, you're doing yourself a favor. If you're in the line of the shot, then even if you can't catch the ball your body may block it from going in the goal.

When an attacker is coming at you straight on, you can still narrow the angle. If it's a one-on-one situation, then you should gradually move off the goal line. The closer you are to your opponents, the narrower their shooting angle. It will also force them to shoot farther away from the goal. Lastly, it puts you in position to scoop up the ball if they happen to dribble it out too far in front of them. Whatever you do, though, don't rush in unless you can be sure of getting the ball. Otherwise, it's sure goal for the other team.

## GET BEHIND THAT BALL

Getting behind the ball means more than just narrowing the angle before the shot is taken. Once you see what type of shot it is, you also have to move your body again, keeping the "behind-the-ball" principle in mind. If, for some reason, you fail to catch the shot, you want your body to be in a position to block it.

This applies especially to a ball coming in on the ground. You must get down on one knee to pick it up. If you take the lazy route and bend over from a standing up position, there's much less of your body around to stop the ball, especially if your legs are apart.

Goalkeeper's first step when moving to a shot

## USING THE HANDS

Once you're in position, it's time for you to use the best asset that you have as a goalie—your hands. You have the privilege of being the only player allowed to use her hands, so be sure to take advantage of it.

Unfortunately, many beginning goalies lose sight of this. They've been recruited from the field for the goalkeeping position and their first instinct is to reach out with their feet to stop the shot rather than to drop down and use their hands. Some new goalkeepers also try to use their bodies to stop the ball first and then catch it once the edge is off the shot. Don't make these mistakes. Your hands and arms should be doing the bulk of the work, but always get your body behind your hands when it is possible. Balls can slip through the hands but not through the body.

As the goalie you must always have your hands up with your thumbs behind the ball. This will allow you to absorb some of the velocity of the kick. Do not try to scoop the ball into your chest. There's no give that way, and chances are the ball will bobble around and possibly bounce out.

Sometimes a ball can't be caught because it is out of range. In this situation, you need to punch or push the shot wide or over the top of the goal. Punch the ball when it is within easy reach. Push it with your fingers if it's

Hand position: thumb-to-thumb above waist

Hand position: pinky-to-pinky below waist

Fist punch

Finger push at maximum reach

almost out of reach. Make sure that this happens. The last thing you want is to punch the ball in the goal or to punch it right back in front of the goal, thereby giving the other team a better shot. By knocking the ball out of bounds, you may give the other team a corner kick, but at least that gives your defense a chance to get in position. If there are no attackers right in front of the goal, this is the one time you can choose the option of slapping it down in front of you.

## DIVING

Diving is the most difficult skill a goalie has to learn. It goes against any natural instinct you may have. The problem, you see, is that you have to dive on the ground without using your hands to break your fall. Your hands have to be free to catch the ball. Any goalkeeper who uses her arms or hands for landing is going to be in trouble. By the time her hands are done breaking her fall, the ball will be in the net.

Just as important as learning how to dive is learning how to avoid diving. If you have learned the best place to stand when an opponent is coming at you, you have a better chance of being in the right place to block the shot. The more experienced you get at reading a shot, the less you'll have to dive. Take a look at the top goalkeepers in the sport: When they're playing, it looks as though the shooters are always hitting the ball straight to them. In reality, it's just that the goalies are always in the right place.

## AFTER THE SAVE

Once you have saved the ball, you have to get it back out to your teammates. You can do this in three different ways: rolling, tossing, or punting. There are advantages and disadvantages to all of these methods, but no matter which one you choose, you should get the ball out to the sideline rather than down the center.

If you have picked up the ball on one side of the goal, that sideline is the one you should roll, toss, or punt to. You almost never want to cross the ball in front of the goal. If something should go wrong, you would be out of position, and the opponents would have an open goal for the taking.

If you receive the ball in the middle of the goal, however, you have both sidelines as options. As a general rule, you probably want to switch sides of the field. As often as players are told not to bunch, the majority will have shifted over to the side of the field from which the ball came. If you switch sides, it may allow your receiving player a few uncontested moments, during which time she can settle the ball and set up some good passes.

Even if there isn't an imbalance in the field, it's good strategy to alternate the sides of the field. The more unpredictable a goalie is, the harder it will be for her opponents to get a handle on where the ball will be placed.

## The Roll

When deciding which option—roll, toss, or punt—to use, look at your teammates. A roll is good when the other team has backed way off and one of your teammates is wide open near the goal. The roll will be accurate and easy to handle, and your team's offense can begin.

The roll is like a quick bowling move, minus the ready position up in front of the face. It should be powerful and accurate, leading your teammate by only a few feet.

## The Toss

If there's no one open within rolling range, look for a teammate to toss the ball to. This will most likely be a wing defensive player who has moved out to the sideline. A toss is better than a roll because it will get the ball farther away from your goal, although it won't be quite as easy to handle because it will be coming out of the air, rather than rolling on the ground. Never toss the ball unless there's someone open to throw it to. You don't want to throw the ball merely because it's an easy option. It could be stolen and come right back in your face, especially if one of your defensive teammates is still hanging out on the wing.

The toss most goalkeepers favor is a wide-arm swing using just the one throwing arm. Given the size of the soccer ball, this type of throw will get the ball to go a longer distance than a baseball throw. And a one-handed throw provides more momentum than a two-handed one, thus giving the goalkeeper a little more power and, therefore, a little more distance.

## The Punt

If your best option seems to be punting the ball, your goal will be to get it as far down the field as possible; it's much harder to guarantee that you will get it to your teammate with this option. First, punting is not as accurate as rolling or tossing, and second, the long loft time will allow your opponents time to move into position to guard the receiving teammate, even if she was open at the start of the punt. With this in mind, the length of the punt becomes vital. You want to get it as far away from

Goalkeepers have an advantage because they can reach up high with their hands.

you as possible in order to give your teammates the opportunity to gain control.

As a goalie, you are not allowed to walk with the ball in your hands, so you can only take a step or two before you kick the ball. This step is important, though, because it gets your body into motion, allowing momentum to contribute to the force behind the punt. This step should almost be a running step or a hop to maximize your power.

Hold the ball out in front of you in both hands. The ball should be low. Then, just before you kick it, drop the ball as your foot comes up to meet it. Don't make the mistake some beginning goalkeepers make of tossing the ball up before the kick. This dramatically reduces your accuracy and power. The kick should always be with the instep, and your toe should be pointed.

Unless you have a very powerful kick that can get the ball to the center of the field, you probably want to kick it off to the side. This will make it easier for you to defend against a lost punt. Your teammates should be aware of this and should already be spread out and in position to receive the ball on the wing when you go to punt. Try to choose an open teammate, although chances are she will be covered by the time the ball gets to her.

# GAME SITUATIONS

After all the individual skills have been worked on, you need to practice being a goalkeeper under all types of game situations. Ending each field drill with a shot on goal will help both you and your field-playing teammates. Full scrimmages will obviously provide conditions close to those in matches, but even small-sided games such as a three-on-two or a five-on-three situation will help you learn how to move in the goal and how to direct your defense. There should be plenty of this activity during practice sessions.

On top of that, you need to practice special situations. Set up corner kicks, direct kicks, indirect kicks, and penalty kicks, and make sure you know where you should stand and where your defense should stand in order to best block the goal.

## Corner Kicks

Every goalkeeper dreads corner kicks, with good reason. The opponents get a free kick, and usually it's coming right into the penalty box in front of the goal. On top of that, the opponents often bring practically their entire team down to be available to receive the kick. As a result, your whole team comes down to play defense, and the result is chaos. It's your job to shout out orders to tell your team where they should be.

With this in mind, stand on the far post, away from the kick. This will not only enable you to see more of the action, but it will give you the easier task of moving in on the ball to catch it, rather than moving backward.

If you know you're going to be able to catch the ball, yell "Mine!" or "Goalie!" so your teammates will know to get out of your way and let you catch it. You'll still have to contend with the bodies of the opponents, but if you reach up with your hands and jump in the air, you should have an advantage over them.

Position for the corner kick: Face the kicker and place one hand on post

© Infobase Publishing

## Direct Kicks

Direct kicks are free kicks that are taken from outside the penalty box.

They can go straight into the goal. Because the kicker is unopposed and can take her time placing the shot, she will have an easier time finding an open space in that monstrous soccer goal. To simplify your job of defending that huge, gaping space, turn your defense into a wall, blocking the portion of the goal directly in front of the kicker. According to the rules, the wall must

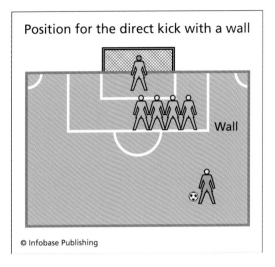

Position for the direct kick with a wall

Wall

© Infobase Publishing

be at least 10 yards away from the kicker, but don't let your wall give her any more room than that.

The best way to line up the wall is to make sure the outside shoulder of the outside defensive player is lined up with the outside post of the goal, thereby completely blocking one side. That way the kicker can only go around the wall in one direction. On that side, the shot is your responsibility, but since it's a much smaller area to cover, this shouldn't be too difficult. You'll also have to watch out for the ball that is lofted over the wall, but if the wall is close enough to the kicker, the shot will have to be awfully loopy and slow to get over it, which should give you plenty of time.

## Indirect Kicks

Indirect kicks are similar to direct kicks in that they are free shots on goal, but they must touch another player first. For this reason the wall is ineffective. You never know which player will be taking a shot, and you don't want your entire defensive team lined up in front of the wrong player. The best defense against indirect kicks is for you to move with the ball and pray that your defense marks up tightly.

## Penalty Kicks

There are rigid rules in soccer defining how a goalie should defend against a penalty kick. The ball is placed on the hash mark that is located in front of the goal, 12 yards out. The shot is a contest between the shooter and the goalkeeper. The rest of the players must stand outside the penalty box until the shot has been taken.

The goalie must start with both her heels on the goal line until the ball is kicked. Only then is she allowed to move. The goalie is definitely at a disadvantage, so basically the best she can do is keep her eyes on the ball and hope for a bad shot.

Some goalkeepers try to anticipate where the ball will go by noticing which foot is dominant and remembering how the player has shot the ball in the past. Then, with a preconceived notion of where the ball is going, the goalie can prepare to spring to that side as the ball is being kicked. If the goalkeeper has guessed wrong, however, it's a sure bet that the ball will score on the other side, because the shift back will take more time. Also, a goalie has to be careful not to telegraph which way she might be going by leaning in that direction.

# DRILLS

## Learning to Dive

To learn to dive, you should start on your knees. This way you will learn the proper fall without having too far to go. It will be easy to master the skill if you're not afraid of hurting yourself. Have another goalie on your team toss balls to either side of you and fall on them as if you are diving.

Learning to dive

Once you have gained confidence in the amount of falling abuse your body can take, stand up and do your dive without the ball. Build up a feel for this harder diving without worrying about catching or blocking a shot.

Finally, you'll be ready to add the ball. Notice that once the ball is introduced, you're no longer just falling to the ground; you're actually diving toward it. This is important because if you just fall you will be too late. The person feeding you the ball should mix it up: dives to the right, dives to the left, and also some balls that can be saved standing up.

## Reflexes

In general, you're either born with quick reflexes or you're not, but reflexes can be improved upon, and a goalie must work on them daily to make sure she's performing at peak level. This drill takes care of that.

Two goalies should kneel opposite each other about five feet apart. Then it's time to "play catch." The idea is to throw the ball as hard as possible at the other goalie and vary the placement of the throw each time, making sure that it is always within reach. Balls should be in the air and on the ground. This is a great drill for endurance, too.

## Rapid Fire

This is a drill that everyone loves and one that's good for a goalkeeper's endurance as well as her skill development. Each field player should take a ball and players should line up at the edge of the penalty box. When the goalkeeper is ready, the first player takes a shot. As soon as the ball is just about at the goal, the next player takes a shot, and so on down the line. Timing is important here. The shooters don't want to give the goalkeeper much time to recover, but they do have to be realistic and not fire all the balls at once, or it won't be a helpful exercise.

The first time through this drill, players should aim for the goalie. In this way the keeper can warm up by making contact

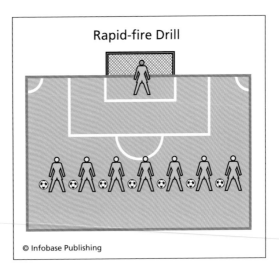

Rapid-fire Drill

© Infobase Publishing

with every single ball without having to fly all over the place. Once she's warmed up, the players can start aiming for the edges.

## Shuffle, Touch, and Layout

**Number of Players:** 1 player plus coach
**Equipment:** soccer ball, 5 cones
**Playing Area:** field

The key to fast reflexes in the goal area is proper footwork. Proper footwork gives you balance, which allows you to move quickly to your right, left, forward, and back. This drill helps develop footwork, specifically the moves needed for making diving saves.

Set up five cones in a "Y" shape. The first cone should lie in the middle of the goal, two feet in front of the goal line. The second cone stands two

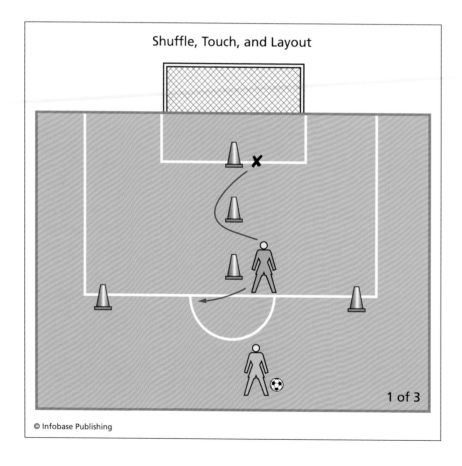

Shuffle, Touch, and Layout

1 of 3

feet in front of the first and the third two feet in front of the second. Two more cones are set up to form the tips of the "Y" shape (see diagram).

The goalkeeper starts by shuffling through the first three cones. Make sure she keeps her knees bent and body low to the ground. After shuffling through the second and third cone, she moves quickly to the cone to her right and touches it with her right hand. As she touches the cone, the coach kicks (or volleys) a ball toward the cone directly to her left. She attempts to make a diving save.

After making the save, she rolls the ball back to her coach, backpedals to the goal line, and starts again. Repeat this four or five times. She should switch to touch the left cone with her left hand so that she practices diving to the right as well.

**Shuffle, Touch, and Layout**

2 of 3

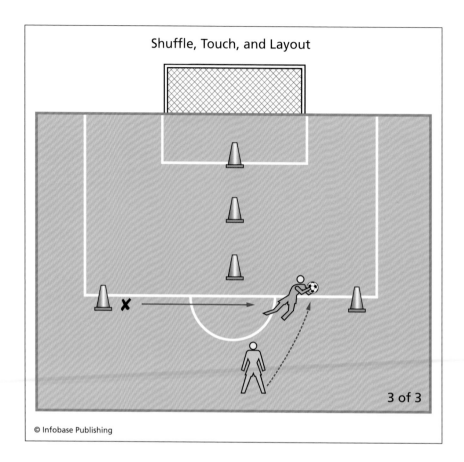

Shuffle, Touch, and Layout

3 of 3

© Infobase Publishing

# GAME TIME

## Goalie

**Number of Players:** 2–4
**Equipment:** soccer ball
**Playing Area:** wall or small area with goal marked

Goalie is a great game to play at a wall or someplace where space is limited. Players should mark off one section of the wall or playing area as the goal. One player will be the goalie. She stands in front of the goal area and does her best to keep the ball from going into the goal. The other player works on her shooting skills and tries to get the ball past the goalie. If she succeeds, she gets a point. If the goalie makes a save, she throws the ball back out to the other player, who must kick the ball before it stops moving. After 10 tries, the players switch positions. The player who has the most goals at the end is the winner.

If there are several players shooting on the goal, they take turns. It's a good idea to draw a boundary line to keep the shooters far enough away from the goal so the goalie doesn't get hurt by a ball coming in too fast.

# 10
## Tactics

In 1986, John Cullen, the women's soccer coach at Bowdoin College, was in his second year of coaching when he found his team making it to the final game of the conference tournament. It was a good team, but not a great one, and Cullen knew that Bowdoin's competition—Bates College—had an excellent team. Bates also had the home-field advantage and a lot of fan support.

"I knew if we got there the traditional hour before the game to warm up, my players would get intimidated," remembers John. "So rather than do that, I stopped at a high school field about five minutes from the Bates campus. We did our stretching and warm up drills, got back on the bus and got to the field a few minutes before the game was going to start. My 20 players filed off the bus with one ball, kicked it around a little and were ready to start. It completely threw the Bates team off and took away the effect of their crowd. We went on to win 1–0."

Tactics like Cullen's aren't the norm when a coach or players are figuring out a way to win a game, but paying attention to small details like this could mean the difference between a win and a loss.

A coach should be concerned with every aspect of the team. He or she needs to know the physical strengths and limitations of the players, their strategic expertise, and their degree of mental toughness. And it doesn't hurt to know a few of these things about your opponents as well.

Strategic know-how is crucial for the players, too, because unlike in other sports, such as softball or basketball, the coach isn't calling the plays. Once a soccer player is out on the field with the ball, it's up to her to create opportunities. Often a good head game can compensate for weaker skills.

# EMBRACING OFFENSE AND DEFENSE

When soccer players describe their positions, they often say, "I'm a defensive player" or "I'm an attacker," but the truth is that every player should consider herself both an attacker and a defender. This is the most important tactical philosophy for a coach to impart to a team.

If a fullback does her defensive job and steals the ball away from the opponent, she should then consider herself on offense and place herself in the best position to help attack the goal. A good attack starts at the very moment a team gains the ball, not when the ball crosses the center line or gets near the opponent's goal. Teams who remember this have a real advantage because at turnover time many of the opposing players are likely to be in bad defensive positions.

And that statement should be a strong reminder to all forwards. The situation is reversed. If you're a forward and the other team steals the ball from you, don't stand there moping. You want to go after the opposing players with everything you've got; you're on defense now. Why let the ball travel all the way down the field if you can quickly turn the play around at your end? Every player should be in the game at all times, and if a team can embrace that philosophy the rest is gravy.

# POSITIONS

When developing an overall strategy for your team, you need to examine the strengths, weaknesses, and abilities of your players. You want to place players in positions that capitalize on their strengths and you want to have a formation that compensates for any possible weaknesses your team may have as a whole.

While there are 11 players on a team, there are only four basic positions:

1. fullbacks (or defenders),
2. midfielders (or halfbacks),
3. forwards, and
4. the goalkeeper

With the exception of the goalkeeper, the number of players in each position varies with the team strategy, and all players are expected to pass well, defend well, and play both offense and defense. Nonetheless there are some general duties associated with each position.

The fullbacks are expected to defend the goal from the opponent's attack. If they do their job well, the goalie won't ever have to make a save.

The Four Basic Positions

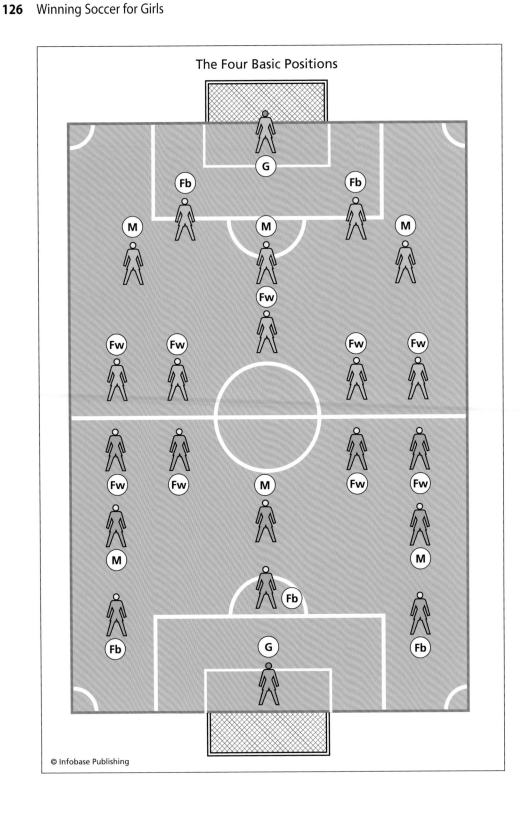

The fullbacks intercept the ball, block the attackers' progress, and "tackle" (essentially getting your foot on the ball and stealing it) when the situation merits. Because fullback must defend forwards, these defenders must have speed.

The midfielders, also called halfbacks, are the links between the forwards and the defenders. They coordinate the play on the field. They should be superior passers, long-distance runners, and able to play both offense and defense effectively.

The forwards' primary responsibility is to put the ball in the goal. To do this, they need to be proficient shooters, dribblers, and headers. Speed is helpful, too, for breakaways and beating the defenders, especially when the defenders lack speed.

# FORMATIONS

In soccer's early years, before the rules were formalized, the popular formation was to have nine attackers, two defensemen, and no goalie! This strategy has obviously changed drastically—over the years it seems that coaches have been developing formations that have continually reduced the number of attackers. Despite this, the formation you choose for your team should depend less on what setup is trendy at the moment and more on the strengths of your particular players.

Once you've figured out who is best on attack and who is best on defense, you have to put them together in a cohesive team. There are a number of accepted formations, and all can be effective if they're used appropriately.

A lot depends on the team, but all formations include a certain number of fullbacks, a certain number of midfielders, and a certain number of forwards. The goalkeeper is never mentioned in the formation descriptions because there is always only one. The other 10 players, however, can be mixed and matched depending on the strengths of the team. Here are some of the most popular:

1. **4–3–3.** This setup is used more than any other, and it actually looks more like a 1–2–1–2–1–2–1 than a 4–3–3. There's a sweeper back in front of the goal, two wing fullbacks on the side, a stopper in front of the sweeper, then two wing midfielders on the side. The center midfielder is pushed up near the forwards, who are two wings and a striker. This formation is popular because all areas of the field are covered solidly.

   Leslie Orton, the former women's soccer coach at Williams College in Williamstown, Massachusetts, found that the best way to impart the concept of the 4–3–3 was to compare it to one of those collapsible

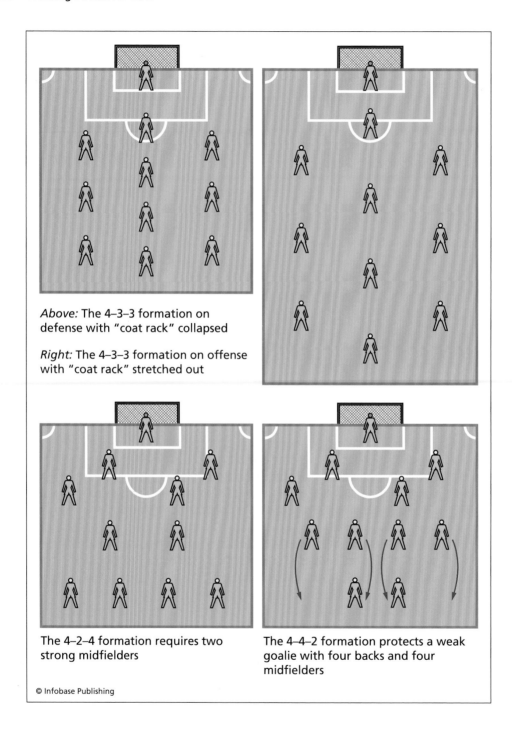

*Above:* The 4–3–3 formation on defense with "coat rack" collapsed

*Right:* The 4–3–3 formation on offense with "coat rack" stretched out

The 4–2–4 formation requires two strong midfielders

The 4–4–2 formation protects a weak goalie with four backs and four midfielders coat racks. "When the team is on offense, the coat rack is all stretched out, creating a series of diamond shapes. As the team is pressured back on defense, the formation collapses and the positions become more of a straight line across. In other words, the fullbacks are in line with the fullbacks, the midfielders with the midfielders, and the forwards with the forwards."

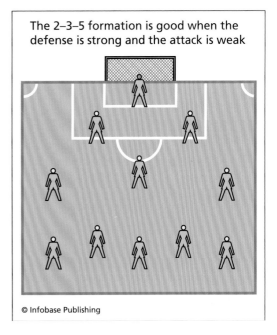

The 2–3–5 formation is good when the defense is strong and the attack is weak

© Infobase Publishing

2. **4–2–4.** This formation is clearly weak in the middle, but it has the advantage of overloading both the offense and the defense. It's a good formation to use if the team has two strong midfielders who are in great shape. The midfielders have to link the offense and the defense as usual, which means covering a lot of territory up and down the field, but now they also have to cover half the field widthwise. Overlapping by the fullbacks does take some of the pressure off, though, and provides an extra dimension to the offense.

3. **4–4–2.** If your goalie is weak, this is the formation to use; hopefully the four fullbacks and four midfielders will prevent the ball from ever getting to the goal. However, it obviously has its drawbacks on attack. In this formation, as in the 4–2–4, overlapping is the key, and all four midfielders participate.

4. **2–3–5.** This formation was standard years ago, but it is not very popular anymore because most teams don't feel comfortable with such a weak defense. There are five forwards in this formation: the center, two inners, and two wings. The inners hang back a little and help out the midfielders, and the center midfielder hangs back a little and helps out the fullbacks. This is good for a team with a couple of outstanding defensive players but weak forwards; it creates a stronger attack out of sheer numbers provided the forwards maintain adequate spacing. This is also called the W–M formation because of the shape it makes on the field.

# OFFENSIVE STRATEGY

Soccer is such a low-scoring game that if you score a goal, you're likely to be the star of the game. Scoring is the glamour part of soccer and what everyone focuses on, but what most people don't realize is that the shot is the final tiny piece in the offensive puzzle. While the picture would be incomplete without it, many other pieces have to come first. And it's this sound offensive strategy that makes a winning team.

Soccer doesn't have specific plays, the way basketball and football do, but there are some general concepts that all offenses should try to execute:

1. **Get the ball to the center when you're in the opponent's half of the field.** With the ball in the center, you have more passing and shooting options, with the choice of going either left or right. The defenders also won't be able to cut off your shooting angle as easily. If you're on the side, on the other hand, the sideline will do half of the defenders' job for them. Now they just have to block your pass in to the middle of the field.
2. **Spread the defense.** The more area the defense has to cover, the harder it is for them. Therefore, if the people the defense is covering are all over the field, the defenders have their work cut out for them. If, on the other hand, the offense is all bunched in the middle, the defense can stay there, too. Spreading the defense has the additional advantage of keeping the middle somewhat clear, which gives your shooters a little more room to maneuver.
3. **Support the player in front of you.** If you're a fullback or a halfback, don't think your job is over once you've passed the ball to your forwards. Stay behind them and let them know you're there, because they may need to pass back.
4. **Switch fields.** If all the play has been on one side of the field for a while, try moving the ball to the other side. Your opponent's entire defensive unit has to shift, and if they don't do it quickly, it may provide the opening you need.

# DEFENSIVE SKILLS AND STRATEGY

When you're on defense, all your efforts should be focused on protecting the goal. It stands to reason that the more players you have in defensive positions, the more easily you will be able to accomplish this. That's why it's so important for the midfielders to drop back as soon as the opposing team gets the ball.

# Marking a Player

Most teams use a player-to-player defense. You pick up the designated player as she approaches the goal and "mark" her. This means that you want to deny her the ball. Most importantly, you want to place yourself between that player and the goal, but you also want to try to get between her and the ball if you can do that without sacrificing goal protection.

You don't have to be on top of your designated player all the time. The farther she is away from the ball, the farther you can be from her. This allows you to support your teammates should an opposing player break away.

If she does get the ball, you want to apply high pressure. Bother her so much that she can't look up to see what her passing options are. Push her toward the corner of the field, rather than the center. Not only will you be going away from the goal, but the sideline and end line will eliminate two passing and dribbling directions.

Soccer coach John Cullen feels that good marking skills are the key to defense, and he will often have his players work on marking with no ball involved. "When you teach marking," he says, "you want to stress position, movement, and quick feet. If there's no ball, then players can focus on developing these skills."

John feels this is especially helpful with beginning players. "Their offensive skills are in the early stages, so it's often easier than it should be for the defense to get the ball away. Then the defense gets sloppy with their marking because it isn't as important."

Only after players have mastered the marking skills should a ball be introduced, and John has a suggestion for that, too. "We like to do a drill I call Speedball. In this, the offensive players pick up the ball in their hands to pass it, like in basketball. The defensive players have to react a lot quicker when they're marking in Speedball than they would if the offense had to use their feet to move the ball. Then when the defense gets in a real game situation, it seems easy to mark."

# Stealing the Ball

The key to stealing the ball away from an attacker is keeping your eyes on the ball. Don't make the mistake of watching the feet or legs, because a good player will use them to mislead you.

You also want to choose your moment carefully. If you rush in at full speed, it will be an easy matter for the attacker to sidestep you. An effective way to steal the ball is to run alongside the attacker until you sense your moment. This is when you tackle the attacker.

Stealing the ball

When you attempt a tackle, make sure you choose a moment when you're well balanced. You have to be able to move quickly once you get your foot on the ball, and you can't take time to steady yourself. You should stick your tackling leg in front of the ball and then shift your weight onto that leg.

## Support

Sometimes a player attempts to steal the ball but the only thing that happens is that she's left looking foolish as the attacker dribbles on past her toward the goal. When this happens, the rest of the team has to lend their support. The next player in line should move in, and the defender who was unsuccessful should swing back around to cover the now newly exposed player. All defenders whose players are at least two passes away from the ball should be pulling off their players and protecting the vulnerable middle area. Even if there is high pressure on the player with the ball, the defense will be ineffective if the rest of the players don't cut off the other passing opportunities.

If you find yourself without support and are facing a two-on-one situation, the best thing to do is delay a commitment to either player, hoping that by slowing the attack, you're giving your teammates a chance to recover and lend you support. If you rush in to guard one player instead, the player you didn't choose to guard will have an open goal.

# GAME TIME

## Three on Three on Three

**Number of Players:** 9 (or 11 if you want to have two goalies)
**Equipment:** soccer ball
**Playing Area:** field

Three on Three on Three requires an incredible amount of running, so players who are not in good shape should beware. Players form three teams of three each—Team A, Team B, and Team C. Team A lines up in front of one goal. Team B lines up in front of the other goal. Team C is in the middle. If there are goalies, the regular goals can be used. Otherwise, the goals should be smaller.

Team C starts with the ball. They head down the field in the direction of Team A. Team A is defense and Team C is offense, so Team C will try

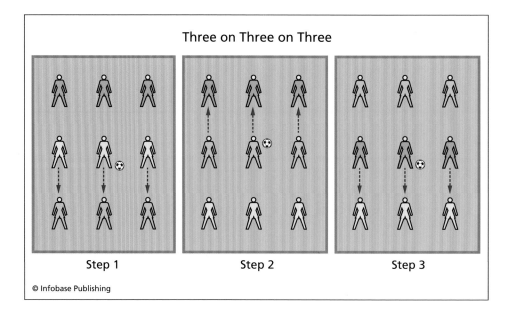

Three on Three on Three

Step 1    Step 2    Step 3

© Infobase Publishing

to score a goal and Team A will try to stop them. When Team A gains possession of the ball, either by stealing it away from Team C or after a Team C goal is scored, they take off down the field toward Team B. Team C stays at the end where Team A was.

Team A is now offense against Team B's defense. When Team B gets possession of the ball, they take off toward Team C. Team B is now offense; Team C is now defense. Play goes for a specified amount of time, and the team that has the most goals at the end of that time is the winner.

## Line Soccer

**Number of Players:** 8 or more
**Equipment:** soccer ball
**Playing Area:** field with two parallel boundary lines

Players divide into two equal teams and stand opposite one another on the boundary lines. The teams count off so that each member of the team has a different number. For instance, if there are five players on each team, the players would be numbered 1 through 5 on one team and 1 through 5 on the other team.

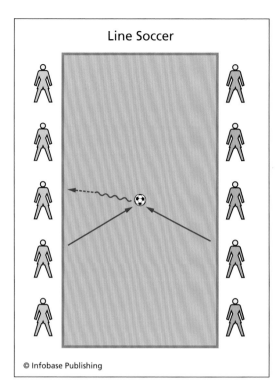

Line Soccer

© Infobase Publishing

The referee or coach or someone who is not involved in the play calls out one or more numbers and throws the ball into the center of the field. The players whose numbers are called must rush out, retrieve the ball, and try to get it across the opponent's line, thereby scoring a point. Obviously, the player from the other team who has the same number will be trying to do the same thing, so it turns into a mini one-on-one game or two-on-two, etc.

The players whose numbers are not called are left standing on the line. They may not leave the line, but they are allowed to block any attempts to get the ball over the line as long as they do not use their hands or arms.

Sometimes all the numbers will be called, which leaves the line more vulnerable; players will have to protect against that.

If a point is scored, the players go back to their lines and the referee calls out different numbers. However, the referee may choose to do this in the middle of the play as well. If the players who are out there get their number called again, they may continue to kick the ball, but if totally new numbers are called, they must leave the ball exactly where it is and sprint back to their line as the new numbers come out to battle.

Play until one team has scored 10 points.

## Square Soccer

**Number of Players:** 4 or more
**Equipment:** one or more soccer balls
**Playing Area:** small square

This game has some similarities to Line Soccer in that the object is to get the ball over the opponent's line. Players are divided into two equal

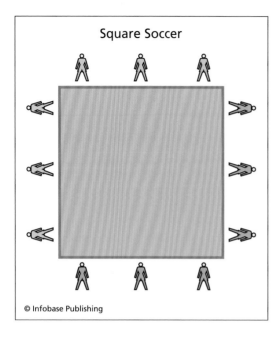

Square Soccer

© Infobase Publishing

teams and are confined to a small square. Each team is responsible for two sides of the square, and the object is to kick the ball over the other team's sides.

Players stand on the edge of the square and do not go into the center. The ball pops back and forth between the teams like a ball in a pinball machine. If the ball does leave the square, the team not defending the side that it crossed gets a point. The first team to score 15 points wins. If many people are playing, more soccer balls can be added to make the game more challenging.

## Monkey in the Middle

**Number of Players:** 3 or more
**Equipment:** soccer ball
**Playing Area:** anywhere

The object of Monkey in the Middle is for two players to retain possession of the ball for as long as possible while the third player tries to get it away from them. Players may not use their hands, but they may pass the ball, juggle it, chip it over the other player's head, or dribble it away. There are no boundaries.

When the middle player finally does get control, she switches places with the player who lost the ball in the first place. Now that person becomes the monkey in the middle.

If there are more than four players, it is a good idea to have more than one monkey: three on two, four on two, five on two, six on three, and so on. With larger groups of players, it also might be advisable to create boundaries.

## Cone Ball

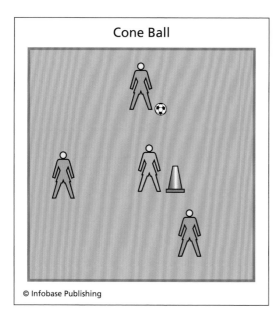

© Infobase Publishing

## Cone Ball

**Number of Players:** 4
**Equipment:** soccer ball and a cone
**Playing Area:** small circle with cone in the center

Cone Ball is similar to Monkey in the Middle, with a variation. Like Corners, this game is three against one. The difference is that while the three on the outside want to keep the ball away from the person on the inside, this is not their primary goal. The object is to hit the cone in the center of the circle. The person on the inside does her best to prevent this. By quick passing across the circle, players may be able to catch the defender on the wrong side of the cone and be able to get off a shot.

If the player on the inside gets the ball away, she changes places with the person she stole it from. If a player hits the cone, she gets a point and then goes into the middle. The player with the most points at the end of the game is the winner.

## Foosball

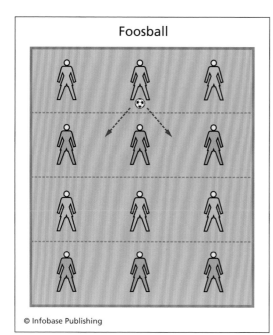

© Infobase Publishing

## Foosball

**Number of Players:** 12 or more
**Equipment:** soccer ball
**Playing Area:** field with four zones carefully marked

Foosball is a game in which players count passes instead of goals. There are four zones on the field. Team A is in zones 1 and 3, and Team B is in zones 2 and 4.

The teams try to pass the ball through the opponent's zone and back again, without the opponents touching the ball. Every time a team is successful doing this, it scores a point. No one is allowed to leave her zone. Each team may pass within its zone as much as it wants to, trying to catch the defense out of position.

Players on a team should switch zones periodically (when play is stopped, of course) to allow all players to play in the more challenging middle zones, where both defense and offense are important. To add more excitement, you can also add another ball.

Play until one team scores 10 points.

# 11
# Restarts

When a foul is committed, when a goal is scored, or when the ball goes out of bounds, someone gets the blame (or credit, in the case of a goal) for having touched it last, and the other team gets possession. That's called a restart. The rules of soccer, however, are very particular about how that ball gets back into play, and they specify that a different type of restart should occur for nearly every situation.

At the beginning of each half and after a goal is scored, the restart is called a kickoff. For balls that go out of bounds, throw-ins, goal kicks, and corner kicks come into play. Direct kicks, indirect kicks, and penalty kicks occur after a foul. A drop kick occurs in a few special situations.

This chapter covers these specialty kicks and throws by showing and explaining what they are, how to execute them, and what players should be doing both defensively and offensively.

## KICKOFFS

A kickoff occurs at the start of the game, the start of the second half, and after a goal has been scored. The team that did not kick off at the beginning of the game is the one that kicks off the second half. The team that did not score the goal is the one that kicks off after a goal has been scored.

The kickoff begins in the center of the field. Each team must remain on its side of the field, behind the center line, until the ball is touched. In addition, the team that is not kicking off must remain outside its half of the center circle, effectively keeping the players 10 yards away from the ball.

The ball must move forward over the center line first, it must travel at least the length of its circumference (i.e., one rotation), and the initial kicker can't touch it again until another player has touched it. After that the ball may move back over the center line and anyone can touch it as many times as she likes.

## Offensive Strategy

Because your entire team is behind you on the kickoff, a big kick forward will just turn the possession over to the opponents. A better plan is to work the ball sideways and backwards until people begin to move into position.

Many teams will start a kickoff with two people close together near the ball. The first player has the job of setting the game in motion by kicking the ball at least one circumference forward. This should be in the direction of the second player, who will be the real playmaker.

Two popular options at this point are kicking the ball out to one of the wing players or kicking the ball back to the center midfielder. The other options the second player has are either kicking the ball back to the first player or taking it up the field herself. Because the opponents will most likely be rushing in on the kickoff, these two options are usually not very effective.

If the ball is kicked to one of the wing forwards over on the sideline, she may want to consider passing it back to her supporting midfielder, rather than trying to battle the concentrated defense in front of her. Maintaining possession, at this point, is a more realistic goal than progressing forward, at least until players move into the attacking half of the field. This is also why some teams are fond of passing back to the center midfielder.

An overlap by one of these midfielders is another good option. Essentially, the wing forward and the midfielder switch roles. While the wing forward is busy receiving the ball, the midfielder can be sprinting down toward the goal to give the wing someone to pass to. This means, however, that the fullback needs to back up the wing in case she needs support behind her.

## Defensive Strategy

Most coaches have at least three attacking players up on the edge of the circle, rushing in the moment the ball is touched or, technically, the moment the ball has traveled its circumference. Usually the offensive team will manage to get the kickoff moving before the defense can get there, but it never hurts to be on top of things in case there is a bungled kickoff.

Also, if the offensive team is going to be passing back to the center halfback, these rushers can just keep on running back to pressure her. That gives them two opportunities to take advantage of the other team's poor kickoff execution.

Unlike these front-line rushers, the rest of the team should be prepared for a successful kickoff and should be covering the players who might receive a pass. The wing forwards are likely targets, and the defense should be spread out near them accordingly. They also have to be careful not to leave the middle open, however, because if the attackers manage to avoid the three front people rushing in, they may just dribble and use short passes to come down the center.

Because the two teams aren't spread out much yet, and because they are so concentrated on their own sides of the field, the defense usually has a little more success in stopping the attack than the attackers do in getting to the goal.

# THROW-INS

When a player kicks a ball over the sidelines the other team inbounds it with a throw-in. This is one of soccer's odd little quirks. Given that one of the distinguishing features of the sport is that hands aren't allowed to be used, it seems odd that a throwing method would have been chosen to inbound the ball.

In keeping with the anti-handball karma of soccer, however, the restrictions governing a throw-in make the toss very unnatural:

1. The two hands must be used equally. If there's any spin to the ball, the referee will say that one hand was more dominant and the throw-in will be declared illegal, giving the other team the opportunity to throw the ball in.
2. The ball must go over the head in a straight line. If you want to throw the ball at an angle, you must turn your entire body that way.
3. The ball must be released while it is over the head.
4. Both feet must be on the ground at the moment the ball is released.

A coach in any other sport—softball or basketball, for example—would be horrified at the thought of a ball being thrown this way, but those are the rules. Because of this, players have come up with a few tricks to get more power and leverage, since the two-feet-on-the-ground rule keeps them from stepping into the throw. The most common of these tricks is to take a running start and drag the top of the back foot along the ground at the release, but people have even gotten as crazy as doing a front flip to send the ball sailing.

The throw-in

A throw-in is taken from the point along the sideline where the ball went out. The player throwing the ball in must keep both of her feet behind the line until the ball is released. She may not touch it again until another player has touched it.

## Offensive Strategy

While the referee will blow the whistle to let you know when the ball has gone out of bounds, there are no follow-up whistles to tell you when it's time to throw the ball back in. The ball is back in play when you release it. Many teams try to use this fact to their own advantage by moving the throw-in along as quickly as possible before the defensive team has a chance to get in position. Nonetheless, it is far more important to have a good throw to one of your teammates than to inbound the ball quickly, so don't make this a blanket policy if no one on your team is open or available. A throw-in is basically a free pass, and you don't want to waste it.

The throw should be aimed at your teammates' feet, because that will make it easier for them to get it under control. Another option is throwing the ball ahead of your teammate down the sideline. If you have a strong throw and can send the ball flying over the heads of the defense, you can also

Both feet must touch the ground at all times

surprise them by flinging the ball to a teammate in the middle of the field. It won't be long before the defense catches on to your strength, though.

If you are a receiving player, you should be moving constantly, trying to get free. Even if you feel you're in a good position—say, down the sideline—you won't get the ball if a defensive person is hanging all over you. If you do your best to lose her, it will be more likely that you'll receive the ball.

A final tip is to use your inbounder. Many defensive teams forget to mark her, leaving her wide open once the throw-in is made. A good strategy is to do a quick one-touch pass back to her as soon as she steps in bounds. If she's unmarked, she'll have time to set up a more effective attack.

## Defensive Strategy

Defensively, players want to mark up in a player-to-player coverage as quickly as possible. The sidelines are particularly vulnerable and therefore a popular place for throw-ins, so it's also wise to have a back-up defense person down the line. That way, if the pass is down the sideline, over the defender's head, there will be someone else to pick it up. Often, just the presence of another defensive player will be enough to force the throw into the middle.

If the throw does go in the middle, watch for a quick shift to the other side. If everyone is bunching around the throw, the other side will be wide open for attack. Also, a player should always mark the inbounder, so she won't be available for a pass back.

# GOAL KICKS

When the ball goes over the end line, it is returned to play with a kick rather than the throw that is used for the sidelines. The type of kick depends on which team was responsible for kicking the ball out of bounds. Goal kicks are used when the ball is kicked over the end line by the attacking team.

The ball is placed on the six-yard line in front of the goal. Most teams place it on the outer corner of the six-yard line, so the ball is as far away from the goal as possible. Any player, including the goalkeeper, may take the kick, but the player who executes the kick may not touch the ball again until another player has touched it first. Also, the ball must clear the penalty area before it can be touched. If the ball doesn't clear the penalty area, the kick is retaken.

## Offensive Strategy

As usual, you want this kick to be a pass to a teammate, rather than merely a big boot away from the goal. Still, power is a factor. Unless a teammate is wide open near the goal, try to get the ball out as far as you can. Also, make sure you kick the ball out to the sidelines. You don't want to give the opposing team any advantage by placing the ball squarely in the middle of your goal area.

## Defensive Strategy

As with the throw-in, the best strategy for the defensive team is to mark up tightly. Because this kick will most likely be in the air, there's a greater chance that it won't be as accurate as a ground pass. Also, you will have more time to react to where the ball is being sent. If you can be quicker and more aggressive than the receiving team, you'll end up with the ball right in front of the goal. Don't forget to get your head involved, too. It just may be your ticket to getting to the ball first.

# CORNER KICKS

A corner kick is awarded when the defensive team kicks the ball over the end line. The ball is then placed on the corner of the field, where the sideline and end line meet, within the corner arc. The arc closest to where the ball left the field is the one that is used, and the corner flag may not be removed during the kick. The defensive team must remain at least 10 yards away, and the kicker, as usual, may not touch the ball again until another player has touched it first.

## Offensive Strategy

The most popular strategy for corner kicks is to loft the ball right in front of the goal. This is the most vulnerable place for the defensive team because they can't cut off any angle. A pass along the ground is no good because a good defensive team will have someone playing short to intercept the ball and to take advantage of a bad kick.

A short ground pass is always an option if a teammate is open. This is an especially good choice if there's no one on the team who can kick the ball hard enough to loft it in front of the goal. A short pass to the top of the penalty box and then a kick to the center can take the place of a loft.

A goal can be scored directly off a corner kick, so some exceptionally talented corner kickers kick the ball with a spin. The kick actually starts out heading toward the center and then turns in toward the goal. Even if the corner kicker on your team is capable of doing this, it's not always the best option. The goalkeeper has an advantage here in that she can jump up and use her hands to stop the ball, so it might be better to loft the ball into the center and then have a teammate redirect it, so it isn't as easy for the goalie to follow the ball.

If you are the receiving player, you will want to get your head in the way of the ball. There will be a crowd in front of the goal and no time for the ball to drop to the ground.

## Defensive Strategy

As with most restarts, the defensive team is going to want to mark up tightly in a player-to-player defense. Someone should also remember to mark the kicker herself. This person can guard against the short pass and pass back and can be there to take advantage of a bungled kick.

Like the attacking players, the defensive players should plan on using their heads to receive the ball. It's almost a guarantee that the first head to get to the kick is going to determine the direction in which the ball goes. No one is going to wait to let the ball drop.

The goalie should be standing on the far post, directing the show. She can see everything that goes on and has the use of her hands, so she should be listened to no matter what.

## DIRECT KICKS

When a foul is committed, a direct kick is awarded to the fouled team. This is a free kick that is taken from the spot where the foul occurred. The ball must be stationary before it is kicked. It may go directly into the goal. The kick can be a pass or a shot on goal, but it can't be a dribble. Someone else must touch the ball before the kicker touches it a second time.

The fouls that cause a direct kick to be awarded are as follows:

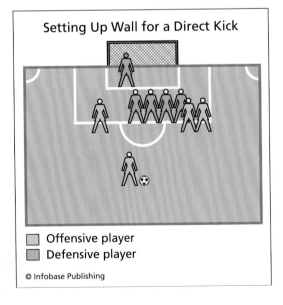

Setting Up Wall for a Direct Kick

☐ Offensive player
☐ Defensive player

© Infobase Publishing

1. Kicking, tripping, hitting, pushing, or jumping on an opposing player.
2. Attacking an opposing player from the rear.
3. Holding an opposing player with the arms.
4. Touching the ball with the hands.

## Offensive Strategy

As with most of the other restarts, there is no whistle to tell you when to start your kick, so the faster you get it done, the more advantage you'll have. Many defensive teams like to set up a wall if the kick is going to be in front of the goal, so if you can get the kick off before the wall is set up, you're in good shape.

If the wall does manage to set up in front of you, you still have a number of options.

1. The four or five defensive players it takes to build a wall guarantees that some of your teammates will be unguarded. A pass to one of them might provide a freer shot on goal.
2. A poorly placed wall might leave one side of the goal wide open. Send your kick there.
3. A wall that is much more than 10 yards away from you is negligible. Loft the ball over the wall and into the goal.

## Defensive Strategy

If the foul takes place within reach of the goal, many defensive teams like to set up a wall. The wall consists of four or five players standing shoulder to shoulder 10 feet away from the ball. Their presence blocks off a portion of the goal and makes the goalkeeper's job a little easier. The goalie knows what is best for her, so she will be yelling at the wall to move left or right if necessary. This advice should be heeded or a wall could hurt more than it helps.

As soon as the ball is kicked, the members of the wall should break up to play defense. You don't want four or five of your players just standing around out of the play. Because of this, a wall is counterproductive when the direct kick is far away from the goal. In this situation, everyone should just hurry back, mark up, and defend.

# INDIRECT KICKS

Indirect kicks are awarded for lesser rules infractions than the ones listed for direct kicks. These infractions are as follows:

1. Dangerous plays—for example, a kick up near a player's face, a kick at the ball while the goalie is holding it, a player lying on the ground and thereby putting herself in danger.
2. Aggressive shouldering when not playing for the ball.
3. Blocking an opponent's path to the ball when not also going for the ball.
4. A restart kicker (or thrower) touching the ball again before another player has touched it.

Indirect kicks are essentially the same as direct kicks, except when near enough for a shot on goal. Then—the reason these kicks are called indirect—the ball cannot go in the goal unless it has been touched by one other player besides the first kicker.

## Offensive Strategy

If your team is taking the indirect kick right in front of the goal, your best bet is to make the first kick a light tap to a teammate standing right next to you (making sure the ball travels at least one circumference, of course). This means that your teammate is the one who is really taking the shot, thereby eliminating the restriction of the indirect kick.

The disadvantage to this play is that the defense is allowed to rush in as soon as the first player has touched the ball. If there is a teammate open farther away, a stronger kick may be preferable.

## Defensive Strategy

Because the ball may be passed to another player, most defenses will not set up a wall to block the kick. Instead, they mark up tightly and hope to get to the ball before the shot is taken.

If the ball has not been touched by a second player and is heading straight into the goal (a rare event, usually occurring only because a player thought she had a direct kick), the goalkeeper is better off just letting it go in rather than trying to stop it. The goal won't count if it goes in untouched, but if the goalie tries to stop it and misses, it will count.

## PENALTY KICKS

Penalty kicks are a goalkeeper's nightmare, but fortunately, they only come into play a couple of times during a soccer season. They occur when a rules infraction that would normally result in a direct kick has been committed in the penalty box by the defending team. Because this foul so close to the goal may have been what prevented the attacking team from scoring, the attackers are given a super advantage: the penalty kick.

This kick is taken by any member of the attacking team. It's a one-on-one kick with the goalie. All other players must stand outside the penalty box until the ball is kicked. The ball is placed on a mark that is centered 12 yards out from the goal. The kicker may take as many steps running in as she wants, but she must kick the ball from that spot. The goalie must begin with both her heels on the end line and may not move until the ball is kicked.

If a member of the defending team commits a rules infraction, such as the goalie moving before the kick or a defensive player moving into the penalty box before the kick, the kick is retaken if the shot was missed. If the shot went in the goal, there is no penalty.

If the kicker commits a rules infraction, such as touching the ball again before someone else has touched it, the defending team gets an indirect free kick.

If another member of the offensive team commits a rules infraction, such as entering the penalty box, the kick must be repeated if a goal was scored.

The defensive strategy was covered in the chapter on goalkeeping. The offensive guidelines for taking the penalty kick are basically the same as in shooting. Try to hit the ball where the goalie isn't. Low balls are harder to save than high ones. And whatever you do, don't miss the goal.

# DROP KICKS

There are a number of different scenarios that would result in a drop kick being taken, yet this type of restart rarely happens. It occurs when the play has been stopped for something other than a rules violation or an out-of-bounds call. The following scenarios are the most common:

1.  An injury.
2.  An erroneous call by the referee.
3.  A damaged ball.
4.  Interruption by nonplayers, balls, or animals on the playing field.
5.  When play has been stopped by a whistle blown by someone other than the referee.
6.  Bad weather or a damaged goal may also stop play, but usually in these scenarios the referee will be able to stop the play at a restart rather than in the middle of play.

A drop kick is taken from the spot where play last ended. The referee drops the ball between two opposing players, who are allowed to kick the ball as soon as it touches the ground. All other players must stand 10 yards away.

# DRILLS

## The Smokescreen

**Number of Players:** at least 10 players
**Equipment:** soccer ball, goal
**Playing Area:** field

Use this drill to practice direct or indirect kicks on offense that are within 30 yards of the goal. In a game situation, a group of players (usually between three and five) will form a wall to protect an area of the goal.

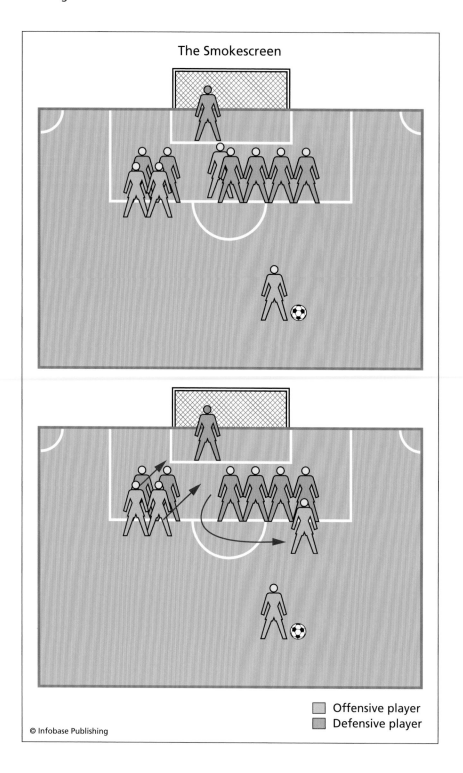

The Smokescreen

Offensive player
Defensive player

# The Smokescreen

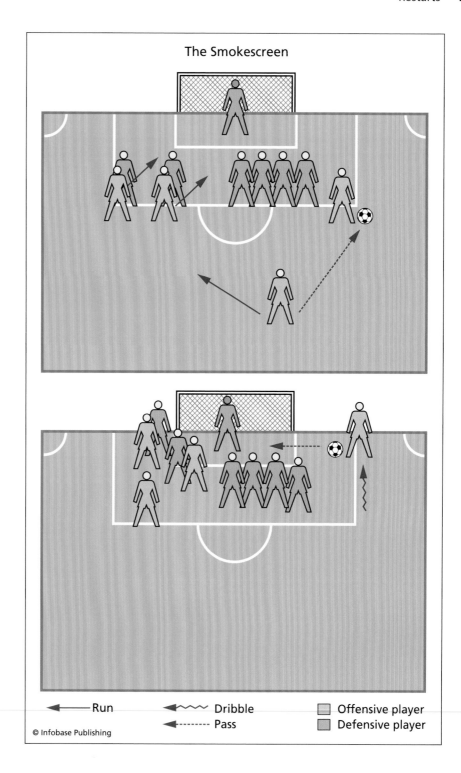

Run ◄──────

Dribble ◄∿∿∿

Pass ◄------

Offensive player

Defensive player

© Infobase Publishing

The wall is set up 10 yards from the ball. (In this case, the free kick is approximately 25 yards out to the right of the goal.) One offensive player stands behind the ball. She is the passer and initiates the play. Another offensive player stands in the wall on the left-hand side. Two more offensive players stand a few yards to the left of the wall (see photo). The rest of the team sets up on the far left-hand side of the field. No players are lined up to the right of the wall. All of the offensive players set up facing the passer.

Standing approximately five yards behind the ball, the passer raises her hand and then drops it. This signals the start of the play. The player standing in the wall breaks to her left and runs across the face of the wall (see photo). The passer approaches the ball as if she's going to shoot. At the last instant, she breaks down and pushes a crisp pass just off the right-hand side of the wall. The player should time her run so that the ball rolls behind the wall before she runs behind the wall toward the goal. If she runs behind the wall before the ball, she'll be called for an offsides violation.

The players standing to the left of the wall break toward the goal and wait for a cross. The passer follows the play.

The girl who runs onto the initial pass gathers the ball and sends a cross in front of the goal. With all the commotion, an offensive player or maybe even several offensive players should be left unmarked—opening up a chance to score.

# 12

# Wrapping It Up

Most people have the impression that soccer is an underdog sport in this country. It's the most popular sport in the world, yet Americans have several other choices when picking a sport to follow. The fact that the United States does not boast a rich history in soccer and no team has ever seriously challenged to win the World Cup makes it difficult to attract the interest of armchair sports fans. That's the bad news. The good news is that none of this pertains to girls' soccer. In fact, more girls play soccer in the United States than in any other country.

Fortunately, there are signs that the boys will eventually catch up. The World Cup was a huge hit when it was finally held in the United States. Youth leagues are immensely popular with both boys and girls. And, finally, the sport is just too much fun to be ignored.

The beauty of soccer is that it is one of the simplest games to learn but one of the most complex games to learn to play well. Not only do players have to master skills, but they have to master strategy as well. A player lacking good soccer sense is lacking one of the most vital skills.

Because players can't rely on preset plays given to them by a coach, they have to develop their own soccer sense—a soccer brain—to help them make the split-second decisions required. This can only happen with experience. That's why it is so important to always play a game during practice, whether it's a full-blown, 11-on-11 game or a smaller five-on-five, for instance. Not only will it help players grasp the big picture, but it will also help point out flaws that wouldn't show up in drills.

For example, you can tell who is supporting on defense and who isn't, who is moving to the open spaces and who is standing still, who is coming to meet the ball and who is waiting for the ball to come to her. You don't

want to find all this out in a real game; you want to find it out in practice when you can stop the action, do it again, and change players' behavior.

Coaches can't afford to let errors go by, no matter how minor. It could very easily mean the difference between a winning team and a losing team. Too often, when their team is losing, coaches ignore the basics and try to develop fancy new strategies, or they shift players all over the field, hoping for a magical combination. More often than not the cure is much simpler: Go back to the basics. Chances are the key is there.

The same advice holds for players. Always work on the basics. Even when you feel you've mastered a skill, keep working on it. Don't worry about developing more complicated moves; just make sure the basic ones are flawless. The goal of every soccer player should be excellence rather than mere competence. The best players in soccer are not the spectacular showmen; they are the ones who practice the simple moves over and over again until they are perfect. The fancy moves will come naturally from improvisation during the game.

Soccer is a game that can be enjoyed on all levels. Beginners find it easy to pick up, yet advanced players still find it challenging. The concept, the rules, and the equipment are simple: All you really need is a ball; you can improvise the rest. But the skills and strategy become increasingly difficult as the level of play increases. The beauty of the sport is that six-year-olds can enjoy it as much as 26-year-olds. Soccer is fast, fun, and challenging. It's no wonder that girls in the United States are leading the way.

# GLOSSARY

**back pass**   A pass to a teammate who is behind the player with the ball.

**center line**   The line dividing the field in half horizontally, behind which each team must remain (on their respective sides) until the kickoff.

**chip**   A short, lofted pass.

**corner kick**   A restart for the offensive team that occurs when the defensive team has kicked the ball over their own end line.

**direct kick**   A free kick, awarded to a team after the opponents foul, that is allowed to go directly into the goal.

**drop kick**   A neutral restart in which the referee drops the ball between two opponents.

**forward**   The position that provides the front line of attack.

**fullback**   The position that provides the last defense before the goalie.

**goal area**   The $20 \times 6$ yard area directly in front of the goal in which the goalie may not be charged.

**goalkeeper**   The defender of the goal and the only player allowed to use her hands.

**goal kick**   A restart for the defensive team that occurs when the offensive team has kicked the ball over their opponent's end line.

**half-volley**   A kick that catches the ball immediately after it bounces.

**heading**   Using the head to redirect the ball.

**indirect kick**   A free kick, awarded to a team after the opponents foul, in which the ball must touch at least one other person besides the initial kicker before it goes into the goal.

**juggling**   Keeping the ball in the air using any legal part of the body.

**kickoff**   The procedure in which the ball is put into play at the beginning of each half and after a goal is scored.

**midfielder**   The position linking the forwards and the fullbacks.

**offsides**   A rule in soccer requiring players to keep either the ball or two opponents (one may be the goalie) between them and the goal.

**one-touch passing**   Redirecting the pass without stopping it.

**overlap**   A run that brings a player who is normally behind up front.

**penalty box**   The $42 \times 18$ yard area in front of the goal in which the goalie is allowed to use her hands and in which the offensive players are awarded a penalty kick if the defensive players foul.

**penalty kick**   A free kick, awarded to a team after the opponents foul inside the penalty box, that takes place between only one kicker and the goalie.

**planting foot**   The nonkicking foot and the one that most influences the flight of the ball.

**square pass**   A pass to the side.

**throw-in**   A restart after the ball goes over the sideline. This is the only time a field player can use her hands.

**volley**   A kick out of the air.

**wall pass**   A two-step pass in which the passer sends the ball to a teammate and immediately receives it back.

**wing pass**   A pass from the center to the sideline.

# SOCCER RESOURCES

**www.us-soccer.com** is the official Web site of the United States Soccer Federation, the governing body of soccer in America. The web site provides information on both the men's and women's national teams, news articles on professional soccer teams and players, and the schedules of the national teams.

*For more information contact:*
U.S. Soccer Federation
1801 South Prairie Avenue
Chicago, IL 60616
Telephone: (312) 808-1300
Fax: (312) 808-1301

**www.usysa.org** is the Web site for US Youth Soccer, which promotes many aspects of the game. There are training tips, health tips, and even advice for coaches.

*For more information contact:*
US Youth Soccer
9220 World Cup Way
Frisco, TX 75034
Telephone: (800) 4SOCCER
Fax: (972) 334-9960

The Web site **www.soccertimes.com** provides a wide variety of information about soccer. There is a section on youth soccer, articles on professional players and coaches, scores of links to many other Web sites, and in-depth information on college teams across the country. To contact the organization, e-mail them at info@soccertimes.com.

Click on **www.fifa.com** to view the Web site of the Fédération Internationale de Football Association (FIFA), the sport's world governing body. FIFA oversees many tournaments, including the World Cup.

*For more information contact:*
FIFA–Strasse 20
P.O. Box 8044
Zurich, Switzerland
Telephone: +41 (0)43 222 7777
Fax: +41 (0)43 222 7878
Email: media@fifa.org

# FURTHER READING

Ascherman, Kurt, and Marco, Stan. *Coaching Kids to Play Soccer.* New York: Simon & Schuster, 1987.

Bauer, Gerhard. *Soccer Techniques, Tactics and Teamwork.* New York: Sterling Publishing, 1993.

Brown, Michael. *Soccer Techniques in Pictures.* New York: Perigee Books, Berkley Publishing Group, 1991.

Coerver, Wiel. *Soccer Fundamentals for Players and Coaches.* Upper Saddle River, N.J.: Prentice Hall, 1986.

Crisfield, Deborah. *The Everything Kids' Soccer Book: Rules, Techniques, and More about Your Favorite Sport.* Avon, Mass.: Adams Media, 2002.

Gallery, Sean. *Soccer Techniques, Tactics and Training.* North Pomfret, Vt.: Crowood UK (Trafalgar), 1992.

Grant, Jack. *Ins and Outs of Soccer: An Illustrated Guide for Coaches, Players and Parents.* Upper Saddle River, N.J.: Prentice Hall, 1992.

Hamm, Mia. *Go for the Goal: A Champion's Guide to Winning in Soccer and Life.* New York: HarperCollins, 2000.

Laprath, Debra. *Coaching Girls' Soccer Successfully.* Champaign, Ill.: Human Kinetics, 2008.

Luxbacker, Joe. *Soccer: Winning Techniques.* Dubuque, Iowa: Eddie Bowers Publishing, 1992.

Maher, Alan. *Complete Soccer Handbook.* Upper Saddle River, N.J.: Prentice Hall, 1983.

Pollock, Robert. *Soccer for Juniors: A Guide for Players, Parents and Coaches.* Indianapolis, Ind.: Macmillan, 1985.

Rosenthal, Bert. *Soccer.* Chicago, Ill.: Children's Press, 1983.

Rosenthal, Gary. *Soccer Skills and Drills.* Indianapolis, Ind.: Macmillan, 1984.

Schellscheidt, Manny, with Wickenden, Deborah. *Youth League Soccer Skills: Mastering the Ball.* North Palm Beach, Fla.: The Athletic Institute, 1989.

Schmid, Sigi, and Bob Alejo. *Complete Conditioning for Soccer.* Champaign, Ill.: Human Kinetics, 2002.

Treadwell, Peter. *Skillful Soccer.* New York: A & C Black UK (Talman), 1992.

# INDEX

Boldface page numbers denote major treatment of a topic. *Italic* page numbers denote illustrations.

## A

Achilles tendon stretch  14
Air Attack drill  56
Akers, Michelle  2
angle, narrowing. *See* narrowing the angle
ankles
    loosening up  14
    for outside-of-the-foot pass  37
arms, stretching  19

## B

back muscles/strength
    for heading  92
    rocker exercise for  23
    Stomach Toss drill for  28
back pass  50, *50*, 155*g*
Back-to-Back, Chest-to-Chest, Head-to-Head drill  25
backward head flick  92
balance, for steals  133
ball  7, 22, 23
ball, keeping eyes on
    for steals  131
    when heading  87
    when passing  31
ball control. *See* control
ball handling. *See* dribbling
ball placement, for shooting  73–74, *74*
basics, importance of  154

Bates College  124
body
    narrowing the angle with  108–109
    trapping with  52–53, *53*
Bowdoin College  124
brain  23–24, 153
breakaway  60
Bull in the Ring game  69–70
Bulls versus Cows game  70
bunching, avoiding  47
butterfly stretch  18, *18*

## C

calf stretch  14, *15*
center, getting ball to  130
center halfback  141
center line  155*g*
center midfielder  140
Chastain, Brandi  3
chest trap  52, *53*
China, ancient  1
chip  35–36, 155*g*
circuits (exercises)  21
communication
    of passing opportunities  47
    for receiving the ball  50
    when goalkeeping against corner kicks  116
conditioning. *See* fitness
Cone Ball  137, *137*
control
    drills for  43–44
    Firing Squad Survival game for  70–71
    and inside-of-the-foot pass  32
    and one-touch passing  38
    when passing  30–31

    while dribbling  61
Controlled Shots (drill)  78, 78–80, *79*
corner flag  145
corner kicks  **145–146,** 155*g*
    goalkeeping against  116, *116*
    and out of bounds  9
Corners game  56, 56–57
crunches  22, *22*
Cullen, John  124, 131
cut back  63, *63*
cuts and fakes  63, 63–64

## D

defense/defenders
    evading  61–63
    and 4-2-4 formation  129
    and overlap pass  49
    spreading  130
    supporting teammates  12
defensive strategy  **130–133**
    for corner kicks  146
    for direct kicks  147
    for goal kicks  145
    for indirect kicks  148
    for kickoff  140–141
    for throw-ins  144
direct kicks  *146,* **146–147,** 155*g*
    foul offense  11
    goalkeeping against  116–117, *117*
    Smokescreen drill for  149
distance running  20–21
diving, for goalkeeping  113, *118,* 118–119
diving headers  91
Diving Headers drill  98–99